Baedeker's

CANADA

How to use this book

Following the tradition established by Karl Baedeker in 1844, sights of particular interest and hotels and restaurants of particular quality are distinguished by either one ★ or two ★★ stars.

To make it easier to locate the various sights listed in the "A to Z" section of the Guide, their co-ordinates on the large country map are shown in red at the head of each entry, e.g. Montréal **H 16**.

Only a selection of hotels and restaurants can be given; no reflection is implied, therefore, on establishments not included.

The symbol ⓘ on a town plan indicates the local tourist office from which further information can be obtained. The post-horn symbol indicates a post office.

In a time of rapid change it is difficult to ensure that all the information given is entirely accurate and up to date, and the possibility of error can never be completely eliminated. Although the publishers can accept no responsibility for inaccuracies and omissions, they are always grateful for corrections and suggestions for improvement.

Preface

This guide to Canada is one of the new generation of Baedeker guides.

These guides, illustrated throughout in colour, are designed to meet the needs of the modern traveller. They are quick and easy to consult, with the principal places of interest described in alphabetical order, and the information is presented in a format that is both attractive and easy to follow.

This guide covers the whole of Canada and also includes the Waterton Glacier International Peace Park, the major part of which is in the north-west of the United States of America.

*Crossing
Canada by train*

The guide is in three parts. The first part gives a general account of the country, its political and geographical divisions, its landscape, climate, flora and fauna, population, educational systems, government and administration, economy, history, famous people, art and culture. A number of suggested itineraries provide a transition to the second part, in which the country's places and features of tourist interest – towns, provinces, regions, rivers – are described. The third part contains a variety of practical information. Both the sights and the practical information are listed in alphabetical order.

The new Baedeker guides are noted for their concentration on essentials and their convenience of use. They contain numerous specially drawn plans and colour illustrations; and at the end of the book is a large map making it easy to locate the various places described in the "A to Z" section of the guide with the help of the co-ordinates given at the head of each entry.

Contents

Nature, Culture, History
Pages 10–95

Facts and Figures 10
General 10 · Geography 12 · Climate 23 ·
Flora and Fauna 32 · Conservation 38 ·
Population 41 · Religion 46 · Education
and Science 49 · Government 51 ·
Economy 55 · Transport and
Telecommunications 61

Sights from A to Z
Pages 98–561

Abbotsford 98 · Acadia 98 · Alaska
Highway 100 · Alberta 102 · Algonquin
Provincial Park 106 · Annapolis Royal 107 ·
Annapolis Valley 109 · L'Anse aux
Meadows 111 · Ashcroft 112 · Athabasca
River 113 · Baffin Island 114 · Baie
James 117 · Banff National Park 119 ·
Banks Island 128 · Barkerville 129 · Bas St-
Laurent 130 · Bathurst 131 · Batoche
National Park 132 · Battleford 133 ·
Bonavista Peninsula 134 · Brandon 136 ·
Brantford 137 · British Columbia 137 · Burin
Peninsula 141 · Cabano 142 · Calgary 143 ·
Campbell Highway 153 · Campbellton 154 ·
Canmore 155 · Cape Breton Island 156 ·
Caraquet 159 · Cariboo Highway 160 ·
Charlevoix 164 · Charlottetown 165 ·
Chilliwack 167 · Churchill 168 ·
Cochrane 169 · Columbia River 170 · Côte
Nord 171 · Crowsnest Highway 172 · Cypress
Hills Provincial Park 181 · Dawson City 183 ·
Dempster Highway 187 · Edmonton 188 ·
Ellesmere Island 198 · Estrie 199 · Flin
Flon 201 · Forestry Trunk Road 201 · Fort
Carlton 202 · Fort Langley 203 · Fort
MacLeod 203 · Fort McMurray 205 · Fort
Providence 206 · Fort St James 207 · Fort St
John 208 · Fort Steele 208 · Fraser
Valley 210 · Fredericton 213 · Fundy
Bay 217 · Gaspésie 220 · Georgian

Practical Information from A to Z
Pages 564–631

Air Travel 564 · Bears 565 · Bed and
Breakfast 568 · Bus Travel 568 ·
Camping 569 · Canoeing and Rafting 570 ·
Car Rental 572 · Currency 572 · Customs
Regulations 573 · Cycling 573 · Diplomatic
Representation 573 · Electricity 573 ·
Emergencies 574 · Events 574 ·
Ferries 577 · Filming and Photography 578 ·
Filling Stations 578 · Fishing 579 · Food and

Index 632

Principal Sights 638

Imprint 640

Large map of Canada at end of book

4

History 63

Famous People 69

Culture 77

Art History 77

Suggested Routes 85
TransCanada Highway 85
Round Tours by Car 90
Rail Journeys 92
Coach Tours 95

Bay 223 · Glace Bay 226 · Glacier & Mount Revelstoke National Park 227 · Golden 229 · Grasslands National Park 230 · Great Bear Lake 231 · Great Slave Lake 231 · Gros Morne National Park 232 · Halifax 234 · Hamilton 240 · Hay River 242 · Hope 242 · Hudson Bay 244 · Hull 245 · Icefields Parkway 247 · Îles de la Madeleine 251 · Inside Passage 252 · Inuvik 253 · Jasper National Park 255 · John Hart–Peace River Highway 259 · Joliette 262 · Kamloops 262 · Kingston 265 · Kitchener-Waterloo 267 · Klondike 269 · Kluane National Park 271 · Kootenay National Park 272 · 'Ksan 275 · Labrador 277 · Lac La Biche 281 · Lac Megantic 281 · Lac St-Jean 282 · Lake of the Woods 282 · The Laurentians 283 · Lesser Slave Lake 285 · Lethbridge 287 · Lloydminster 288 · London 288 · Louisbourg 290 · Lunenburg 291 · Mackenzie District 292 · Mackenzie River 293 · Manitoba 295 · La Mauricie 300 · Medicine Hat 301 · Mission 302 · Moncton 302 · Montréal 305 · Moose Jaw 321 · Moosonee 322 · Muskoka 323 · Nahanni National Park 323 · New Brunswick 325 · Newfoundland 327 · Niagara 334 · North Bay 340 · Northern Woods and Water Route 343 · Northwest Passage 341 · Northwest Territories 343 · Nova Scotia 347 · Nunavut 380 · The Okanagan 352 · Ontario 357

· Orillia 361 · Oshawa 362 · Othello-Quintette Tunnels Historic Park 362 · Ottawa 363 · L'Outaouais 374 · Peace River 376 · Peterborough 377 · Point Pelee National Park 378 · Portage la Prairie 379 · Prescott 380 · Prince Albert 380 · Prince Albert National Park 381 · Prince Edward Island 382 · Prince George 389 · Prince Rupert 390 · Pukaskwa National Park 391 · Qu'Appelle Valley 392 · Québec (Province) 393 · Québec (City) 397 · Queen Charlotte Islands 415 · Regina 418 · Repulse Bay 422 · Réservoir Manicouagan 423 · Revelstoke 424 · Rideau Canal 425 · Riding Mountain National Park 426 · Saguenay 427 · Saint John 429 · Saint John River Valley 434 · Saint John's 436 · St Lawrence Waterway 439 · Saskatchewan 442 · Saskatoon 447 · Sault Ste Marie 449 · Selkirk 452 · Sudbury 453 · Tadoussac 456 · Terra Nova National Park 457 · Thunder Bay 457 · Timmins 460 · Toronto 461 · Trois-Rivières 477 · Truro 477 · Upper Canada Village 478 · Vallée Richelieu 479 · Vancouver 480 · Vancouver Island 498 · Victoria 510 · Victoria Island 517 · Waterton–Glacier International Peace Park 518 · Welland Canal 522 · Whistler 524 · Whitehorse 524 · Windsor 527 · Winnipeg 528 · Wood Buffalo National Park 537 · Yellowhead Highway 539 · Yellowknife 551 · Yoho National Park 553 · Yukon Circle Route 557 · Yukon Territory 557

Drink 580 · Getting to Canada 581 · Golf 581 · Hotels and Motels 583 · Hunting 599 · Indians and Inuit 600 · Information 600 · Insurance 602 · Language 602 · Lodges 602 · Measurements 602 · Medical Services 603 · Opening Hours 603 · Outfitters 603 · Parks, National and Provincial 603 · Post 604 · Public Holidays 605 · Public Transport 606 · Radio and Television 606 · Rail Travel 606 · Ranch

and Farm Holidays 607 · Restaurants 610 · Roads 617 · Shopping 621 · Sport 622 · Taxes 622 · Taxis 623 · Telephone 623 · Time 623 · Tipping 624 · Traffic Regulations 624 · Travel Documents 626 · Walking and Trekking 626 · When to Go 627 · Winter Sports 628 · Youth Hostels 629

Baedeker Specials

Helpmate and Sporting Companion 342

Vive le Québec – libre ... 398

Brazil of the North 502

Call of

Red-White

flashes come from the lighthouse on Prince Edward Island

Tourism has advanced dramatically in the last few years. In 1996 of the more than 17 million foreign visitors to Canada, nine out of ten were from the United States. But also many Europeans cross the broad Atlantic every year eager to experience the immensity of the American north and follow in the footsteps of trappers, fur traders and gold prospectors. Research shows that for many visitors, wilting from endless hassle, stress and lack of space, Canada is the travel destination of their dreams. Vast forests, thousands upon thousands of lakes, boundless prairies, oceans of corn, magnificent high mountains, glaciers glinting in the sunshine, beautiful unspoilt coasts and an exceptionally varied flora and fauna, act like a magnet. At the same time, with its post-modern glass skyscrapers, vast shopping malls, and multi-lane highways, Canada also embodies the opposite extreme. People rave about its big cities, those in the east not lacking in history, those in the west seeming to have sprung from the ground in just a few decades.

Also, as is only to be expected of the world's second largest country, Canada displays immense cultural diversity, from "Miss Saigon" in Vancouver and Toronto and "Anne of Green Gables" on Prince Edward Island, to the renowned Red Indian carvings. In the spheres of architecture, painting, literature, theatre and music, Canadian creativity can only be marvelled at. Douglas Cardinal,

Pure Nature

Imposing rock scenery of the Gaspé Peninsula

Pure Culture

Ambitious architecture of the Museum of Civilization in Ottowa

the North

Mosche Saved, Tom Thomson, Emily Carr, Margaret Atwort, Leonard Cohen, Gratien Galinas, Glenn Gould ... the list is endless. And, as if scenic wonders such as Niagara Falls and the Athabasca Glacier, and cultural highlights such as Québec Old City, the great Ottawa and Toronto art collections and the world-famous totem poles in Stanley Park casting their spell on every visitor were not enough, there are major technical achievements to be admired, such as the CN Tower in Toronto and the huge hydro-electric plants in Labrador.

Added to all this are the seemingly inexhaustible possibilities for activity holidays, everything from whale watching and trekking to exhilarating trips by canoe or kayak, not to mention the quiet joys of fishing in tranquil mountain lakes.

Canada's long tradition of multi-culturalism is reflected in the country's rich mosaic of nationalities. The Vikings are known to have settled on the east coast of Canada at the turn of the last millennium. A few centuries later the English, French, Spanish and Portuguese arrived on the scene. Then, in the 19th and 20th c., Germans, Poles, Ukrainians and many others set forth in their numbers en route for the "Promised Land".

Whether as new homeland or simply a place to spend a holiday, Canada casts an irresistible spell.

Amusing

view of the "Ursus maritimus" of Hudson Bay

Totem Poles

The pinnacle of wood-carving art of the NW Coast Indians

Nature, Culture History

Facts and Figures

Foreword

Canada has long enjoyed great popularity as a holiday destination. World famous natural beauty (the Niagara Falls and the impressive mountain scenery in the Banff and Jasper National Parks are just examples), immense areas of vast countryside, but also the cities rich in tradition such as Québec and Montréal and the vibrant developing cities including Toronto, Calgary, Edmonton and Vancouver with outstanding examples of modern architecture are all worth the journey. Canada has something for everyone – for those who enjoy strolling around town centres, lovers of nature and wildlife or those seeking adventure.

In the limited space of this volume only a selection of the countless sights of interest to the visitor in this vast North American country can be included.

General

Location

Canada, the second largest country in the world, with an area of 9,970,610 sq. km (3,848,655 sq. mi.) (the largest being Russia, 17 million sq. km (6.6 million sq. mi.)), occupies the northern half of the North American subcontinent. The most southerly point of Canada is latitude 41°41'N, the most northerly point 83°7'N, the most easterly longitude 52°37'W and the most westerly 141°W. This vast country stretches over approximately 5500 km (3417 mi.) from the Atlantic to the Pacific Ocean (six time zones). From Ellesmere Island in the north to the Niagara Falls in the south is a distance of 4600 km (1840 mi.). Its area is comparable to that of Europe as far as the Urals. Canada's highest point is Mount Logan (5951 m (19,531 ft)) in the north-west.

Economy

Canada belongs to the world's leading economic nations. An enormous wealth of mineral and vegetable resources, fertile land for agriculture and forestry along with an immense potential for hydro-electric power have contributed to Canada becoming one of the world's leading economic powers. Practically all minerals essential to modern industry can be extracted in Canada. This North American country ranges among the world's leading producers of potash, nickel, zinc, copper, gold and iron.

This gigantic country possesses considerable quantities of coal, oil and gas (especially in the province of Alberta). Water power, available in excess, is harnessed by the huge hydro-electric stations. Providing enormous amounts of energy (particularly electricity) to the neighbouring USA contributes to the Canadian export surplus.

Hydro-electricity constitutes about 70 per cent of electricity produced in Canada. Almost 50 per cent of the country is covered in forests. The boreal pine forests, which stretch from the Atlantic far into the northwest (Yukon), are an almost inexhaustible source of wood pulp and cellulose for the paper industry. Two-fifths of the world's newspaper comes from Canada! The forests in the west, where there is more rainfall, provide the best quality wood for felling and building in large quantities.

Not much more than 7 per cent of the country is suitable for agriculture. Yet the Canadian Prairies, where four fifths of Canada's arable land is found, are one of the most important granaries in the world. In the west of Canada cattle rearing and fattening take place on a vast scale. Milk production is concentrated in the St Lawrence Lowlands where vegetable growing is also important.

◀ *The Athabasca Glacier*

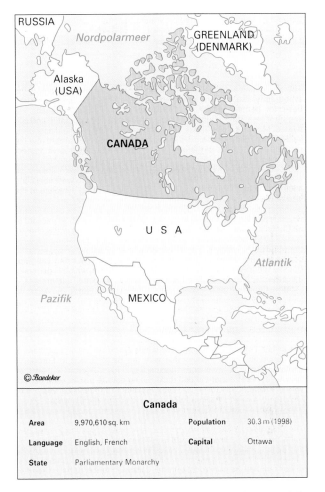

RUSSIA
Nordpolarmeer
GREENLAND
(DENMARK)
Alaska
(USA)
CANADA
U S A
Atlantik
Pazifik
MEXICO
© Baedeker

Canada			
Area	9,970,610 sq. km	**Population**	30.3 m (1998)
Language	English, French	**Capital**	Ottawa
State	Parliamentary Monarchy		

Canadian industry is highly developed. Technology and research in the areas of energy production, mining, forestry and food production as well as telecommunications and transport have earned international prestige.

More than four fifths of the total area is uninhabited. In sharp contrast the population is concentrated in an almost 500 km (310 mi.) wide strip in the south of the country, parallel to the US border. Almost 80 per cent of Canada's population live here. Two thirds of all Canadians are concentrated in the south-east of the country (southern areas of Ontario and Québec provinces), especially in the highly industrialised areas – Toronto-Hamilton–London–Windsor and in the conurbation of Montréal. Other densely populated areas are the Edmonton–Calgary axis in the plains of the eastern slope of the Rocky Mountains, around the Pacific

Population

11

harbour of Vancouver, the region around the capital Ottowa and the St Lawrence Lowlands with the historical city of Québec.

Geography

The geographical framework of Canada encompasses the geology, the topography, the soil, the rivers and lakes, the climate, and forms the basis for human settlement. The extreme conditions in Canada are apparent from only 11 per cent of the total area being populated and cultivated. Minerals, soils, rivers, lakes and woods have potential economic value. These natural resources influence both human settlement and the economy but the size of the country also determines their development and economic value.

Six time zones with between 3½ and 8 hours difference from Greenwich Mean Time, a distance of 5500 km (3417 mi.) from east to west coast and 4600 km (1840 mi.) from north to south provide striking evidence of the size of the country. Five different zones of "northerness" are identified according to the degree of development: the Central Zone or Okumene which is divided into four by mountain ranges and in which 90 per cent of all Canadians live, the Near North which directly adjoins it and is characterised by the boreal wood with little settlement apart from mining towns, the Mid-North, which is almost completely uninhabited and essentially comprises the Yukon Territory, the Northwest Territories and Labrador (mostly tundra and forests), and finally the Far North, which is generally inaccessible, heavily glaciated with only very few isolated settlements.

Some Canadian geographers include the Extreme North, the Arctic, in this category.

Geological formation, Ice Age morphology

Canadian Shield
The oldest core of Canada and the whole North American continent is the Canadian Shield, comparable with the Baltic Shield in Europe. It stretches out in a circle from Hudson Bay. This "Ukraton" consists of several layers of ancient folded rocks dating back to the Archean period, with the newest fold being Pre-Cambrian 800 to 1100 million years ago. Over long geological periods of time rock from the Canadian Shield formed part of the neighbouring areas.

Border Lands
The "Border Lands" surround the lowlands and plateaux of the Canadian Shield. They are made up of the Arctic Lowland in the north, the Interior Plains in the west and St Lawrence Lowlands in the south. These tablelands consist of horizontal layers of sedimentary rock, deposited over long periods from the Cambrian to the Tertiary. The Pre-Cambrian stratum below is called the "Buried Platform".

Mountains
This ring of lowlands and plateaux is encircled by an outer ring of mountains interspersed with high plateaux.

Appalachians
This upland ring begins in the south-east with the Appalachians which were formed during the Caledonian (about 450 to 390 million years ago) and Varistian (c. 300 million years ago) periods and, like the Varistian mountains of Central Europe, were later folded.

Rocky Mountains
These older mountains, which only reach heights of around 2000 m (6562 ft), face the Rocky Mountains (Cordilleras) in the west, which are Alpidian i.e. 190 to 2 million years ago, are similar to the Alps and were formed from the Mesozoic to the Tertiary periods. The Laramic and Nevadian mountain formation was most significant here with mountain chains and enclosed plateaux.

The third outer ring of mountains are the Innuitians in the north, the so-called Franklin Orogen, folded in the Palaezoic period and heavily glaciated owing to their northerly position with high Alpine features.

Apart from the geological structure, i.e. the rock formation, another important element in the shaping of the landscape was glaciation. As in Europe North America was subject to four phases of glaciation. They are the Nebraska Ice Age (beginning 600,000 years ago), the Canada Ice Age (beginning 480,000 years ago), the Illinois Ice Age (beginning 230,000 years ago) and the Wisconsin Ice Age (beginning 72,000 years ago). During the Pleistocene era 97 per cent of Canada's present-day land-mass was covered in ice. The only exceptions were the southernmost parts of Alberta and Saskatchewan and small areas of the Yukon. Almost all evidence of the first three ice ages was erased by the most recent ice age, the Wisconsin Ice Age, which corresponds to our Quaternary Ice Age.

The term "glacial series" refers to the land formations left behind after the ice has melted following a fairly long static period. There is a regular sequence of glacial accumulation (deposition):

1. the icing over inland from north to south left undulating, rounded ground moraines, belts of hilly terminal moraines, sand plains and glacial valleys,
2. the local Alpine-type glaciation left corries, terminal moraines and glacial drift.

With inland glaciation reaching as far as the present-day USA the prevalent form of landscape in Canada is that of ground moraines.

In Canada there were several isolated centres of glaciation. The Laurentide Ice Sheet had such a centre to the east and one to the west of Hudson Bay in Keewatin. The eastern centre divided into various bodies of ice during the Wisconsin Ice Age, which were active independently at times. Among these were the Arctic Islands in the north. The Appalachians were also independently glaciated, and a further large centre of glacial activity was situated in the mountainous zone of the Cordilleras. South of the 48th line of latitude, which roughly corresponds to Canada's southern border, the glacial complexes of the Cordilleras breaks down into smaller complexes.

This perspective shows already that the centres of glacial activity are located in the upland areas because of the wet winters with abundant snow. This applies to the Cordilleras, the Appalachians and also to Labrador, whereas various theories have been discussed regarding Keewatin, which is not of a high altitude.

The terminal moraines are situated just beyond the Canadian Border where older ice ages are identifiable. The Illinois Ice Age near St Louis, on the same latitude as Sicily, pushed south. The main thrust of the Wisconsin Ice Age reached the New York area about 20,000 years ago. Since then the ice has oscillatingly withdrawn and left behind numerous glacial features, as well as a whole drainage network for the meltwater.

Apart from the upper areas of the Cordilleras parts of Baffin, Devon, Axel Heiberg and Ellesmere Islands are permanently covered in snow and ice.

The huge glacial lakes are an outstanding feature, among these Lake Agassiz was by far the largest with an area of 500,000 sq. km (193,050 sq. mi.). This lake, twice the size of Germany, had a maximum depth of 200 m (656 ft). As the ice withdrew it created Lake Ojibway-Barlow with an area of 175,000 sq. km (67,567 sq mi.), i.e. 350 times the size of Lake Constance. Finally, the whole series of Great Lakes belongs to the group of lakes beyond the boundary of the mighty sheets of ice, which were already tectonically formed. Lake Athabaska, the Great Slave Lake and the Great Bear Lake also mark the boundary of former ice sheets.

Hudson Bay underwent great changes and after the post-glacial rise of

Innuitians

Glacial evidence

Centres of glaciation

Glacial lakes

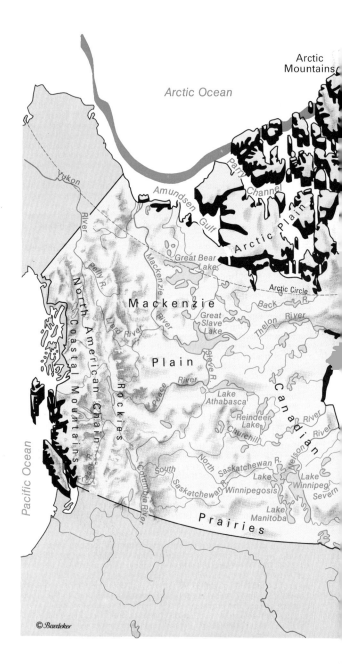

Mountains
Rivers and Lakes

Baffin
Bay

Baffin
Island

Davis Strait

Atlantic

Labrador

Sea

Ocean

Foxe
Basin

Hudson Strait

Ungava
Bay

Hudson

Bay

Labrador

Rivière Caniapiscau

Churchill R.

ain

James
Bay

La Grande Rivière

Appalachians

Cabot Strait

Albany River

Shield

Lake
Nipigon

Lake
Superior

Ottawa River

St Lawrence River

Lake
Huron

Lake
Ontario

Plain of
St Lawrence

Lake
Erie

Geography

On the edge of the Arctic

the land in the south was encircled with a layer of marine clay (Clay Belt). Similarly to the Baltic Shield in Europe the disappearance of the massive ice cover caused an isostatic rise to the Canadian Shield in North America, while the melting of the glaciers led to an eustatic rise in sea level. This interplay of isostasis and eustasis has affected the morphology of vast areas of Canada.

All in all it must be said that the Ice Age has transformed this region. An extensive network of rivers, uneven gradients with fast-flowing rivers and waterfalls are widespread. Drumlins and osers (see below) are to be found in many places, particularly west of Hudson Bay and North Québec. In regions of raised marine clay the soil is fertile as in the Clay Belt.

Drumlins are elongated ground moraines – between 100 m and 2 km long – with a steeply sloping rear side and dropping away gently on the other in the direction of the flow of ice; they have an elliptical outline. They were formed in places where the glacier met an obstacle.

Oser

The so-called "oser" (eskers) are very long embankments, vertical to the edge of the ice, formed by the debris deposited by glacial meltwater before it flows from the glacier, when the glacier is stationary.

Canadian Shield

The Canadian Shield – the dominant geological feature of Canada – encompasses an area of over 5 million sq. km (1,930,501 sq. mi.) and covers about 43 per cent of the total land surface. It stretches as far as the great glacial lakes in the west; its highest points in the east are on Baffin Island and in Labrador. Some of its geological formations date back to the earliest geological periods of time. The characteristic rocks are granite and gneiss, in which grey boulder clay or metamorphised sandstones are present. Conglomerates, sandstones and limestones are not so common.

As granite and gneiss are the most resistant to erosion, numerous flat crests with rocks scraped smooth by the ice and hollows can be recognised. The sea level is relatively low, between 200–600 m (656–1968 ft). The Shield adjoins Hudson Bay, which is surrounded by a clay belt.

Hudson Bay itself has only an average depth of 100 m (328 ft) and a maximum depth of 230 m (745 ft) and was therefore subject to severe changes caused by the isostatic and eustatic fluctuations. Former beaches can be easily identified indicating a phased withdrawal of the sea. The debris from weathering which had accumulated in hollows was cleared out by the ice and the rock crests worn down.

Hudson Bay

Although the Canadian Shield is of little agricultural value, its mineral wealth, its giant forests and water power are of great importance to the economy. The minerals comprise chiefly metal ores, but asbestos, spar, mica and graphite are found. The most important reserves, according to output, are iron, nickel, copper, zinc, gold, uranium, platinium and silver. The mines are situated on the southern edge of the Shield and were discovered from the 1890s onwards with the development of the railways. Other sites are in the north-west of the Canadian Shield and in the Labrador-Trog with its iron reserves. The many deep rivers with their numerous falls were ideal rafting routes, today they are used as sites for hydro-electric power stations.

Mineral wealth

The "interior plains" are bordered by the Canadian Shield in the east, the Cordilleras in the west and in contrast to the Canadian Shield are the ideal wheat-growing region of Canada. They stretch from the Arctic Ocean over 2600 km (1615 mi.) to the border with the USA and in the south are turned over to fertile land for cultivation. They occupy about 15 per cent of Canadian territory. The underlying rock consists of massive sediments, deposited on the base rock of the Shield which slopes gently to the east. Devonian and chalk series are most common, where the abundant reserves of oil and gas are to be found. Strata of chalk and Tertiary material form the final layer of sediment, prevalent in the south and west. The present-day surface was mainly a consequence of the Pleistocene Ice Age when material was deposited in changing forms.

Interior plains

As in the USA the southern area of the Canadian Plains consists of stepped countryside, which has three areas (steppes) clearly separated from each other by two prominent tiers. In the east – bordering on the Canadian Shield – the first area is lowland which is referred to, from south to north, as the Manitoba, Saskatchewan and Slave Lowland with an average height of 300 m (984 ft). Large areas of this fertile lowland were once part of Lake Agassiz and are still subject to flooding today. It is an extremely flat, monotonous landscape with massive delta-like deposits.

Steppes

The lowland is bordered in the west by a prominent tier, the Manitoba Escarpment, formed from harder deposits of chalk. The tier faces east and rises 200–500 m (656–1640 ft) above the lowland, with a height of 800 m (2624 ft) in places. This steppe is broken up by rivers into individual ranges of hills (National Park "Riding Mountains" with a variety of fauna).

Manitoba Escarpment

In the west the Manitoba Escarpment adjoins the Saskatchewan Plain, which rises to a height of 300–600 m (984–1968 ft) and displays a variety of relief. Here are higher areas with undulating ground moraines and extremely flat areas of former glacial lakes (in the surroundings of Regina, for example). The surface is modified by glacial activity with sandy crests, kettle holes, fields of dunes, drainage channels among others.

Saskatchewan Plain

A third tier is formed by the Alberta Plain, which lies at a height of 600–900 m (1968–2952 ft). Its relief is prominent with hilly ground moraines and plateaux, formed partly from Tertiary material.

Alberta Plain

Geography

Cypress Hills
The Cypress Hills in the south are an unusual feature rising to 1470 m (5708 ft) and regarded as nunataks, which were not covered in ice. The Mackenzie Lowland takes over from the Alberta Plain in the north-west, a huge alluvial plain which is drained by Canada's longest river, 4240 km (2634 mi.) long, with a drainage area of 1.8 million sq. km (694,980 sq. mi.).

Economic potential
The Interior Plains are of great economic potential. In the south the soils favourable to agriculture are of particular importance. In the north there are giant forests. There are also abundant reserves of tar sands in North Alberta and of oil and gas in the south. Brown coal and potash are also present.

St Lawrence Lowland
The St Lawrence Lowland only covers 3 per cent of the Canadian land-mass but it is one of the most important areas of the country for the economy. Its geological construction consists primarily of Palaezoic sediments which overlay the Canadian Shield. A special feature are the volcanic intrusions, which occurred during the Mezoic period and now remain as projections in the region. Among these projections is Mont Royal, in the centre of Montreal, at a height of 234 m (767 ft) the most well known. In Southern Ontario there are many examples of resistant Silurian limestone deposits carved into steps.

Niagara Escarpment
The Niagara Escarpment is responsible for the formation of the Niagara Falls and the Niagara Gorge. At Niagara Falls Goat Island separates the Canadian Horseshoe Falls (49 m (160 ft) high, 790 m (2591 ft) wide) from the USA Falls (51 m (167 ft) high, 350 m (1148 ft) wide). Niagara Gorge is 11 km (7 mi.) in length and was caused by retrograde erosion of about 1.4 m (4½ ft) per annum (over the last 200 years).

Minerals
The variety of minerals ranges from smaller reserves of oil and gas to salt, gypsum, limestone, gravel, sand and asbestos. Ancient lake beds provide ideal soils for agriculture. Below the Great Lakes the St Lawrence River crosses the Canadian Shield by a series of waterfalls necessitating the technical extension to the St Lawrence Seaway.

Champlain Valley
The fertile clays of the Champlain Sea are also of importance. It extends from the St Lawrence River through the Champlain Valley to the Hudson and is all that remains today of the Champlain Lake.

Appalachians
Only the most northerly slopes of the Appalachians are inside Canadian territory. They cover an area of 500,000 sq. km (193,050 sq. mi.), yet only cover 4 per cent of Canada. During the Caledonian and Varistian periods of mountain building chiefly old Palaezoic sedimentary rock was folded and metamorphised. Granite intrusions can also be found. Later this region was folded and in the Tertiary broken up into a mosaic of fragments.

Highlands, Uplands, Lowlands
As a result of this development there are numerous morphological units with complicated rock formations consisting primarily of limestones, sandstones, quarzite, conglomerates and granite. There are three distinct areas – the upper mountain ranges, the Highlands – the undulating plateaux, the Uplands – the lower-lying areas, the Lowlands. The highest points are 1268 m (4160 ft) in the Gaspé peninsula, 814 m (2670 ft) in Newfoundland and 532 m (1745 ft) on Cape Breton Island of Nova Scotia. They are continued in the New England states where the highest point in the Green Mountains of Vermont is 1339 m (4393 ft) and the White Mountains in New Hampshire reach 1917 m (6289 ft). The plateaux are on an altitude of between 150 to 300 m (492 to 984 ft).

Below 150 m (492 ft) lie the Lowlands, which include regions of Newfoundland situated on the Gulf, areas of New Brunswick and Nova Scotia including Prince Edward Island. The rounded shapes of the

Highlands were formed during the Pleistocene period when the Appalachians were covered in ice. Another result of the Ice Age were the thin coverings of loam debris in the valleys and coastal plains, the fluvio-glacial deposits, which gave rise to settlement strips in New Brunswick and New Scotland. The Annapolis and St John's Valleys are examples.

The economic importance of the Appalachian region lies in its extensive mixed woodlands which cover 70 per cent of the surface area. The Lowlands and the regions around Fundy Bay and Prince Edward Island offer the right conditions for arable land. The specialist crops in the Annapolis Valley are famous. The coastline with its many bays has numerous fishing ports and some important ports such as St John's, Halifax and Sydney.

Economy

There is a wide variety of minerals but they are not particularly important to the economy. Asbestos is to be found in the Eastern Townships and coal found near Sydney, was extracted back in 1825. Zinc, lead and copper ores occur in the strata of the older Palaeozoic era. Less important are deposits of iron, gypsum, salt, barite and oil.

Minerals

The considerable difference between tides is of economic potential. Those in Fundy Bay reach 16 m (52 ft) and at spring tide 21 m (68 ft) making them the highest in the world.

Tides

The Cordilleras encompass an area of 1.6 million sq. km (617,760 sq. mi.), that is 13 per cent of Canada's landmass. They form part of the gigantic 14,000 km (8699 mi.) long chain which stretches from Tierra del Fuego to Alaska. In Canada they extend for 2200 km (1367 mi.) varying in width from 400 to 800 km (248 to 497 mi.). Since Pre-Cambrian times a geosyncline developed here which was folded during the Alpidian mountain formation from the Mezoic period to the Tertiary. The Cordilleras have a very complicated geological formation with folds, faults, tectonic rising and sinking accompanied by volcanic activity and plutonic intrusions. The Ice Age provided the final layer with glaciation during the Pleistocene period.

Cordilleras

As in the neighbouring USA three zones can be distinguished: the eastern Rocky Mountains, the intermontane high basins and the Pacific coastal mountains. North of the 60th latitude the high mountain chain of the Rocky Mountains becomes a series of high plateaux.

Geographical construction

The Rocky Mountains are bordered in the east by the foothills and in the west by the Rocky Mountains Trench. To the north they become the Mackenzie and Porcupine Mountains. The mountainous zones are formed from folded sediment of the Cambrian and Palaeozoic, with widespread limestones and quarzite. In the foothills Mezoic sandstones predominate. The Rocky Mountains are especially impressive in southern Alberta, where they soar up to 3000 m (9842 ft) above the foothills. The highest mountain of the entire chain is here, Mount Robson 3954 m (12,972 ft). The Mackenzie Mountains almost reach 3000 m (9842 ft), the Porcupine Mountains about 1500 m (4921 ft). The often horizontal strata and glacial evidence can be made out on the massive mountain blocks which differ from the Alps in having less sharp ridges and peaks.

The biggest icefield of the Rocky Mountains is the 337 sq. km (130 sq. mi.) and about 1000 m (3280 ft) deep Columbia Icefield. It feeds three great rivers: the North Saskatchewan River which flows into Hudson Bay, the Athabasca River which joins the Mackenzie River and then the North Polar Sea, and the Columbia River, which ends up in the Pacific. It is apparent that the Rocky Mountains are the main watershed of the continent.

Columbia Icefield

Central Purcell: Mountain range in British Columbia

Rocky Mountain Trench

The Rocky Mountain Trench is a pronounced depression which continues into the region of the Yukon Plateau where there are several faults in the trench in the north-west. It consists of long depressions up to 20 km (12 mi.) wide with steep slopes that are often terrassed. This tectonic feature was deepened by river and glacial erosion and deposited elsewhere by meltwater. Many rivers such as the Cootenay, the Columbia River, the Fraser River among others follow this trench for a while, before escaping laterally through neighbouring mountain chains.

Intermontane Zone

Two plateaux make up the intermontane zone: the Nechako-Fraser Plateau in the south and the Yukon Plateau in the north.

The Nechako-Fraser Plateau lies at a height of about 1200 m (3937 ft) and is filled with glacial deposits, which are dissected by the dammed rivers (Fraser, Thompson, Okanagan) that resemble lakes in places.

The Yukon Plateau, which continues into Alaska, is 1000 m (3280 ft) high and surrounded by mountains more than 2000 m (6560 ft) high. The western part of the Yukon Plateau is unusual in that it was not glaciated.

The Yukon Plateau is drained by the Yukon River and its tributaries which in parts cut in up to 600 m (1968 ft) deep. The breaking away of the ice often leads to massive flooding.

Coastal mountains

The Pacific chains of the Cordilleras border the interior basin zone in the west. Three longitudinal zones can be distinguished: the coastal mountains on the mainland, the outer mountain ranges on the offshore islands, which run into the St Elias Mountains on the mainland and the trench lying between both chains including the narrow strip of coastal lowland.

Interior ranges

The interior zone is divided by the extreme northern part of the Cascades, the Pacific and Kitimat chains and the Boundary Mountains on the border with the Alaskan Panhandle. It continues into the Alaska

Range, where Mount McKinley is the highest mountain in North America at 6193 m (20,318 ft). In contrast to the Rocky Mountains the Pacific Mountains are predominantly made up of granite and gneiss. There are many volcanic deposits and intrusions. Sharp ridges, jagged peaks and heavy glaciation are common characteristics of these coastal ranges.

The outer range of mountains begins on Vancouver Island, stretching north to the Queen Charlotte Islands and the Alexander archipelago, including the St Elias Mountains on the mainland. This range, reaching heights of 2200 m (7217 ft) on Vancouver Island, 1000 m (3280 ft) on Queen Charlotte Islands, culminates in the St Elias Mountains with the highest point in the whole of Canada (Mount Logan 5951 m (19,524 ft)). The Elias Mountains are surrounded by massive ice-fields from which surge huge glacial rivers.

Outer ranges

Individual glaciers have joined together to cause glaciation in the foothills. The 42 km (26 mi.) long Malespina glacier which stretches as far as Alaska is one of the largest and most famous in the world.

The parallel ranges of the coastal mountains surround a depression known as the coastal trough. It runs from the Puget Sound between the mainland and the islands and includes the coastal lowland. This depression is also one of the most important areas of settlement in the far west of Canada, because it is at its widest on the north and south side of Vancouver Island and is enlarged in the south by the Fraser River and its delta.

Coastal trough

The geological make-up of the Cordilleras would be incomplete without the inclusion of the frequent earthquakes and the volcanic activity. Large areas of the intermontane basins are covered in lava, which rose from separate chimneys during the Miocene and Pliocene periods. There are 150 active volcanoes in British Columbia and the Yukon region for the Quaternary. They are mostly shield volcanoes but with some smaller volcanic peaks running along the lines of weakness. The last lava eruption is said to have taken place around 200 years ago in northern British Columbia. At present there are no active volcanoes in the Canadian Cordilleras. However, Mount St Helens, which erupted in 1980, is situated not far south of the US border in the state of Washington.

Volcanic activity, earthquakes

As in the Appalachians the forests are an important economic resource in the Cordilleras, covering 70 per cent of the area with valuable species such as fir, spruce and cedar. Another important resource is the wealth of fish in the coastal waters and the waterfalls on the rivers favour salmon fishing. There are only relatively narrow strips of land along the coastal depression suitable for agriculture on the lower reaches of the Fraser River and in the Okanagan Valley with its well known special crops.

Economy

Minerals are also a source of significant economic potential. Even before the turn of the century the gold reserves attracted numerous settlers to isolated parts of the Rocky Mountains. Nowadays copper, lead and zinc ores play an important role. Iron ore, coal and molybdenum are other important minerals. The hydro-electricity reserves are of great economic value. As the rivers contain a great deal of water because of the high precipitation levels and have high waterfalls the water power can be directly harnessed. A world-famous example of this economic exploitation are the aluminium works at Kitimat.

Finally tourism is of great economic importance, inspired on the one hand by the dramatic scenery with huge mountains, glaciers, lakes and wonderful coastlines and cultural highlights on the other. The towns of Vancouver and Victoria captivate the visitor with their attractive locations. The impressive craftwork of the coastal Indians is recognised throughout the world.

Tourism

Geography

Arctic Lowland

The Arctic region of Canada includes the archipelago of islands north of the mainland, which is separated from the rest of Canada by several waterways including the Amundsen Strait and the Hudson Strait. It falls into the Arctic Lowland which, with an area of 1 million sq. km (386,100 sq. mi.), covers 8 per cent of Canada's landmass. Both regions are divided from another by the Parry Channel.

In the Arctic Lowland there are horizontal sediments of the older Palaeozoic period. Limestones and dolomite overlay the deeper subsoil of the adjoining Canadian Shield. A narrow coastal strip also makes up the Arctic Lowland stretching as far as the Mackenzie delta. It is formed mainly from Tertiary and Pleistocene sands and is characterised by numerous river courses and lakes.

Innuitians

Bordering the Arctic Lowland, which from north to south rises from 100 m (328 ft) to 700 m (2296 ft), are the Innuitians. The range was folded during the Palaeozoic period and consists of two chains, which encircle deeper semi-circular areas. The Innuitians soar over 1000 m (3280 ft) reaching their highest peaks on Baffin Island with a height of 2591 m (8500 ft) and Ellesmere Island with 2926 m (9599 ft). The Innuitians are covered in extensive ice-fields from which single mountains protrude as steep-sloped nunataks.

Glacial morphology

The geomorphology of the Arctic regions is particularly interesting. Pleistocene glaciation and the present-day glaciers created high-Alpine chains of mountains with deeply incised fiords and far-reaching valley systems. The micro relief displays a multitude of small features. There are frost-patterns on the earth with stripes, circles and polygons, each pattern depending on the inclination of the slope.

Thufure

These ice formations created by the high pressure of groundwater producing earth hills are widespread and rely on an ice lens in the centre for their dome shape. These thufure can be 1 m high and 2 m radius and are mostly extensively distributed.

Palsas

Palsas are larger and can be between 2–30 m radius and over 8 m high. They have an ice centre which is protected by an insulating peat cover. If the cover is destroyed the ice centre melts and the hill collapses in on itself. Only hollows remain which fill up with water in summer. The existence of these so-called thermokarst has only recently been the subject of research.

Pingos

The most interesting feature are pingos which occur in large numbers in the Mackenzie delta. They are cone-shaped hills with a radius of over 400m and a maximum height of over 50 m. They were formed by groundwater coming under hydrostatic pressure caused by the advancing permafrost breaking onto the surface. Small craters may form in the pingos as the ice thaws.

Economy

The Arctic region of Canada is not of prime economic importance as the minerals present – coal, gas and oil – can only be exploited at tremendous cost. However, the discovery of oil at Prudhoe Bay in North Alaska (1968) was significant and was continued on Canadian soil to the east. In 1970 larger oil and gas fields were discovered on the Mackenzie delta.

In conclusion the geological and geomorphological construction is relatively distinct. Of a total area of 12.2 million sq. km (4,710,424 sq. mi.) including 2.2 million sq. km (849,420 sq. mi.) of water (Hudson Bay, Gulf of St Lawrence, Arctic Seas) the Canadian Shield comprises 5.3 million sq. km (2,046,332 sq. mi.) (43 per cent), the Lowlands 4.1 million sq. km (1,583,011 sq. mi.) (34 per cent), the Mountains 2.7 million sq. km (1,042,471 sq. mi.) (22 per cent) and the coastal plains 0.1 million sq. km (38,610 sq. mi.).

Climate

Overall Canada has a cold winter climate with long winters and short, temperate summers. 60 per cent of the land area, 75 per cent according to some figures, has average annual temperatures below 0°C (32°F). 70 per cent of the country has mid-January temperatures of below 10°C (14°F) and 30 per cent does not exceed an average temperature of 10°C (50°F) even in July. Only in the populated south of the country is the climate more varied and changes over a small area.

The following factors determine the climate:

1. The northern location – only a small tip of Canada on Lake Eerie reaches 42° north (latitude of Rome). The largest part of the country lies between 48° north (western border with US): and 70° north (mainland coast on the Mackenzie estuary, still south of North Cape in Europe!). The northern location increases the differences in sunlight, daylight and temperature between summer and winter considerably. For over 90 per cent of the country the seasonal temperature range is over 30°C (86°F).

2. The size of the continent: the vast interior of the country is only marginally affected by maritime influences, which is reflected in the continental climate with low rainfall and high ranges of temperature.

3. The surface features: the Rocky Mountains, lying across the direction of the prevailing west winds, act as a barrier to the influence of the Pacific Ocean on the interior, contributing to the formation of the Prairies. On the other hand they favour the north-south exchange of air masses and extreme changes in the weather (e.g. blizzards).

4. The temperature and currents in the adjoining seas: the fringes of the Curo-Shio current, comparable with the Gulf Stream in Europe, bring relatively warm water along the Pacific coast to the north creating even temperatures along the coast and high rainfall in the coastal ranges. On the east coast of Canada the Labrador current, in contrast, brings cold water south; in the whole of eastern Canada and around Hudson Bay, the "ice-box" of North America, the temperatures are significantly lower than those of a similar latitude in the west or in Europe – with far-reaching consequences for vegetation, population and land use.

On the basis of these factors the following climatic divisions can be made:

in the south following each other from west to east:

1. the mild winter-warm summer climate of the Pacific coast
2. the cold winter-dry summer climate of the Prairies
3. the cold winter-warm summer climate between the Great Lakes and St Lawrence River

In the north, which covers the greatest area:

4. the boreal snow-forest climate
5. the polar-arctic climate

The distribution of land and water has an important influence on the temperature. Owing to the vast landmass Canada has a predominantly continental climate. The annual range of mean daytime temperatures extends from 38°C (100°F) in Winnipeg, 44.6°C (111°F) at Yellowknife, sinking to 15°C (50°F) in Vancouver on the Pacific coast. Whereas the January temperatures in Vancouver are on average 2.4°C (36°F), in the Arctic north they sink to 28.6°C (19°F) (Yellowknife) and 32.6°C (26°F) (Resolute). Even close to the coast in Labrador temperatures fall to 22.7°C (9°F) in Shefferville and in the relatively favourable climate of the St Lawrence Lowlands the January temperatures are 8.9°C (16°F) in Montréal and 11.6°C (12°F) in Québec.

Distribution of land and water

Along the Pacific coast a relatively narrow zone enjoys a milder climate caused by the warm Curo Current (Pacific North Equatorial Current). Hudson Bay has the opposite effect acting as an "ice box". On the Atlantic coast the maritime climate of the Gulf Stream is countered by the cold Labrador current, which carries the icebergs as far south as Newfoundland. Whereas the July temperatures, for example, Winnipeg 19.7°C (67°F) and even Yellowknife at 16°C (60°F), are comparable with central European temperatures, the winter temperatures are much lower. This is apparent at Winnipeg in the Prairies, which lies on the same latitude as the German towns Mainz and Frankfurt am Main, but the average January temperature is 18.3°C (−1°F), compared with +1°C (34°F) of the above two towns.

Mountain ranges

The lack of east to west mountain ranges has a significant influence on the climate of Canada. In Europe the Pyrenées, Alps and Dinaric Alps act as the "fur caps" of Spain, Italy and Dalmatia but the wide open spaces of Canada lack such protection. It allows uninterrupted exchange of air masses between north and south to take place, which can transport cold masses south in winter and hot air northwards in summer. The dominant north–south direction of the mountain zones is conducive to this exchange of air causing windward and lee effects in a west to east cross-section of Canada, especially in the Cordilleras. These windward and lee effects are characterised by the precipitation, with heavy rainfall on the western slopes and relative dryness on the eastern side. An example is Vancouver Island, where a 14 year average of 6633 mm (261 in.) was recorded on Henderson Island with a record 8222 mm (324 in.) in 1931. On the other hand Penticton in the rain shadow of the mountain chains in the intramontane zone receives only 296 mm (12 in.) of rainfall and Regina in the Prairies 398 mm (16 in.).

West wind zone

Canada lies in the area of westerlies which are governed by air pressure formations. Such areas of low pressure are found in the Aleutians and near Iceland whereas conversely a flat high is formed in the Arctic. Areas of high pressure are also found near the Azores or Bermuda; in summer they can move north and influence the Pacific coast or eastern Canada.

Cyclonic paths

There are five major cyclonic paths which cross Canada. In the west there are ridges on the Pacific coast, in Alberta the leeward location causes a pronounced "cyclone genesis", brought about by the air masses from the north and south. A further cyclonic path follows the Great Lakes and the St Lawrence Lowlands, another the Atlantic coast in a north-easterly direction. In addition there are Arctic cyclones which rarely reach the lower latitudes.

Blizzards

High air pressure and extremes of temperature often cause dangerous storms which develop in the country itself or come up from the south. Blizzards are the most common, i.e. sudden blasts of cold Arctic air accompanied by snowstorms and wind speeds of more than 40 kph (25 mph). Such a blizzard can last several hours with limited visibility. The Prairies are most affected by them. An example of a devastating blizzard was December 15th, 1965 when there was a snowstorm with speeds of 88 kph (55 mph) and temperatures of −35°C (−31°F). In 1966 in Winnipeg a blizzard reached 118 kph (73 mph) bringing a snow cover of 35 cm (14 in.) in a very short time. When air masses from the south are present sleet and long periods of snowfall can occur.

Hurricanes

Hurricanes which originate in tropical latitudes and, somewhat weaker, cause incessant rainfall on reaching eastern Canada, are particularly dreaded. Examples include Hurricane Beth that brought 300 mm (12 in.) of rain within two days in August 1971, or Hurricane Hazel which caused floods and destruction and even claimed lives in October 1954.

Tornados

Unlike hurricanes tornados occur only relatively infrequently. There are about five per year. But there have been horrific examples: in Regina 41 people were killed and enormous damage was caused in 1912. A tornado in Windsor in 1974 left eight dead.

The "Northern Lights" – an impressive natural phenomenon

The Chinook is a well known local wind, a foehn wind in Alberta. Adiabatically warmed air results in melting snow and a sudden rise in temperature. In Pincher Creek in southern Alberta a temperature increase from −18°C (0°F) to +3°C (37°F) within an hour was recorded.

Chinook

The northern light or polar light appears in the form of ribbons, arches, bundles of rays and crowns and may be red, greenish or bluish-white. It is between 100 to 1100 km (62 to 683 mi.) high at the most, increasing towards the equator. It is created by "corpuscles" (electrically charged particles given off by the sun at high speeds) in the earth's magnetic field being attracted to the poles. On meeting the atmosphere they are ionised by its gases; causing the air molecules to glow. The spectrum mainly consists of atoms of oxygen and bands of nitrogen.

Northern light

The zone of northern light encircles the magnetic North Pole at some distance and is very narrow. Over a cycle of 27 days and in a time span of 11 years a certain periodicity in strength and frequency of appearance can be observed.

Meteorologists assume a worldwide warming of 3°C (5°F) on average over the next 50 to 100 years, which will result in serious changes in the Arctic regions more than anywhere. Whereas a rise of 1°C (2°F) is predicted for the tropics the temperature in the Polar regions is set to rise by 12°C (21°F). The acknowledged reasons for the general warming of the earth's atmosphere are, among others, the increased amounts of carbon dioxide.

Greenhouse effect

Such a development would completely unbalance the sensitive tundra landscape. If the permafrost floor melts rivers of mud will carve out so-called "thermo-limestone scenery". In the short Arctic summers the tundra vegetation still insulates the underlying ground. The dramatic final stage of the process would be the melting of the ice cap.

Climate

As the ozone layer is at its thinnest at the poles, it is here where it can first be destroyed. The influence of sunlight on the increased concentration of fluorochlorocarbons in the upper layer of the mantle of air around the earth results in the release of chlorine atoms which attack the vital ozone layer.

Permafrost

The reasons for the permafrost floor are the limited amount of sunlight, low winter temperatures and a thin covering of snow. The underlying ground is cooled down greatly and the earth only thaws superficially in summer. There is a distinction between continuous and discontinuous permafrost. The continuous covers an area of 3 million sq. km (1,158,301 sq. mi.), which is twelve times the size of Great Britain, the discontinuous an area of 1.3 million sq. km (501,930 sq. mi.). The limits of the permafrost concur with $-1°C$ (30°F) and $-7°C$ (19°F) annual isotherms. The lack of vegetation in the tundra is conducive to cooling. The depth of the permafrost therefore increases northwards reaching 366 mm (15 in.) in the Mackenzie delta, 548 mm (21 in.) in Melville Island, with the depth to which thawing occurs seldom being more than a metre.

The discontinuous permafrost is mostly formed in the forest belt where it is not so cold, the vegetation cover resulting in thawing. Owing to the greater degree of thawing the permafrost is restricted to northern slopes or bogs.

Effects

The permafrost has far-reaching consequences for people. Mining is not possible because of flooding. When laying surface pipelines cold aggregate has to be added to prevent the supports from sinking when the upper layer thaws. Roads are damaged as the frost causes the subsoil to break up and parts of the road sink and airfields become uneven. Houses sink down so that recently a method of building on pillars is being tried to provide circulation of air below the house. Insulation and cooling systems are often effective but electricity and water supplies are continually threatened. Waste and sewage disposal is problematic as biological and chemical breakdown is not possible. Even though many problems can be solved by technology it is at great expense and is a clear disadvantage of the north compared with the southern regions. This becomes extreme during the cold season.

Winter influences human life in many ways. The fight against the cold and storms, against darkness and snow demands a lot of energy. Coupled with this the size of the country brings additional problems. In the towns the houses and shopping malls need to be protected against the frost and weather. Transport is hampered by permafrost in summer and by snow in winter, with snowfalls obstructing traffic in the towns as well. On the other hand winter is the chief travel period in the north as the rivers and bogs are frozen and do not present an obstacle.

Climatic graphs

The following paragraphs examine more closely the climatic details of these climatic zones with reference to graphs taken at typical climatic stations. In the graphs on pages 28/29 the annual range of temperature and precipitation is shown. The months are represented by letters. Temperatures are shown by a red band: the upper limit corresponds to the highest average daily temperature, the lower the lowest night. The mean daily temperature for each month can thus be read from top to bottom with a fair degree of accuracy.

The height of the blue columns indicates how many millimetres of rainfall were recorded on average in each month.

These graphs provide the answers to many of the particular questions of the individual traveller. Some examples: the visitor to Ottawa in the middle of July can ascertain from the upper and lower graph limits of the temperature curve that the night temperatures are as low as in Germany, but the daytime temperatures are 6°C (11°F) higher. However, the visitor to Ottawa in February must be prepared for day time temperatures between -16 and $-9°C$ (3 and 16°F), much lower than in Great

Britain. The precipitation curve is equally informative: the rainfall levels from November to March in Vancouver are twice as high as in central Europe, whereas the temperatures are about the same.

For places between the stations the climatic conditions can be estimated by applying simple rules, which follow.

Six climatic zones can be distinguished on the basis of temperature, precipitation, wind conditions. They are the Pacific coastal region, the Cordilleras, the Prairies, the St Lawrence Lowlands, the Atlantic region and the Arctic region.

Climatic regions

Canada's west coast has a maritime climate with high levels of precipitation and low daily and annual temperature variations. It is comparable with the climate of western Europe and very different from the climate of Canada's east coast (see below). The prevailing west winds carry the warmth from the ocean onto the land. At the same time the air humidity turns to precipitation in the form of rain in the mountain slopes. The amount of rainfall decreases from south to north. It depends heavily on the location on the coast with its fiords, bays, inlets and peninsulas and height. In the lee of the mountains and islands and inside the bays the rainfall is considerably higher than on the outer edges of the coast or high altitudes in the mountains.

West coast (Vancouver climatic station)

No other region of Canada has such mild weather. The temperature band for Vancouver is correspondingly narrow and only curves gently.

There is a distinct range of precipitation with maximum rainfall in winter and minimum in summer. The influence of the Mediterranean climate further south on the Pacific coast is felt here. Heading north the temperatures drop (annual mean temperature in Vancouver 10.2°C (50°F), in Prince Rupert on the north end of the Canadian coast 7.6°C (46°F)). Further north, as far as US territory (Panhandle), temperatures fall and precipitation increases until widespread glaciation is found with glacier tongues forming down to sea level.

There is a more pronounced difference in climate inland than northwards. A narrow strip in the eastern hinterland of Vancouver has a cool temperate climate, comparable with that of the southerly St Lawrence region. Towards the east a cold temperate and increasingly dry climate follows. The climatic station Whitehorse at 65° north and about 300 km (186 mi.) from the coast only experiences 257 mm (10 in.) annual rainfall. In comparison the Rocky Mountains are only partially glaciated.

The damp Pacific air masses are dried out after passing over the coastal mountains and Rocky Mountains, so that on the lee side only scarce amounts of rainfall occur, with the foehn-like sinking of the air masses in the eastern-sloping plains being an additional factor. So Lethbridge only has 439 mm (17 in.) of annual precipitation with maximum amount falling in June. Compared with the west coast the annual and daily fluctuations in temperature are much greater. It can be seen on the climatic graph that the mean daily difference in temperature is about twice as great as in Germany. The actual temperatures can be even more extreme than those given. The absolute minimum for February in Calgary is −45°C (−49°F), the absolute summer maximum +35°C (+95°F). Nobody should underestimate the possible fluctuations in daily temperatures or those from one day to the next. When planning outdoor activities this must be taken into consideration with regard to equipment. The absolute lowest night temperatures in Lethbridge, even in summer, up to July, are below freezing. In May and again in September temperatures below −10°C (14°F) have been recorded, a factor being the tremendous heat loss on clear nights. However, the weather is the dominant influence on temperature fluctuations: east of the Rocky Mountains new areas of low pressure form which move west.

Prairies (Lethbridge climatic station)

Each low sucks up air masses from the south on its front, cold air

Climate

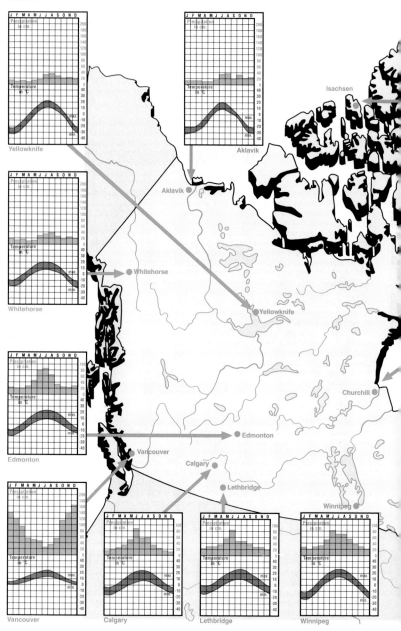

Yellowknife

Aklavik

Whitehorse

Edmonton

Vancouver

Calgary

Lethbridge

Winnipeg

Isachsen

Aklavik

Whitehorse

Yellowknife

Churchill

Edmonton

Vancouver

Calgary

Lethbridge

Winnipeg

28

Thirteen typical regional climatic stations in Canada

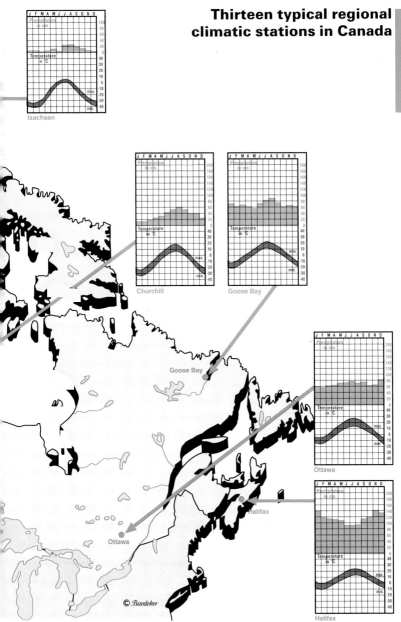

Isachsen

Churchill

Goose Bay

Goose Bay

Ottawa

Halifax

Ottawa

Halifax

© Baedeker

Climate

masses from the north on its back. The exchange of air from north to south can, unlike in Europe, take place unhindered east of the Rocky Mountains. At the extreme it gives rise to winter blizzards with drops in temperature of over 20°C (68°F) in a few hours disrupting traffic and economic activity, occasionally claiming lives, but also heatwaves of tropical air. As crops sensitive to the frost are not grown in Canada the effect of the blizzard on agriculture is not so damaging as in the south of the United States.

In this climate prairie grass turns to hay in the dry autumn, which with quickly falling temperatures is preserved under a thin covering of snow (minimum winter precipitation), whereas in the wetter east it rots or freezes. In earlier times this hay was the preferred diet of the great herds of buffalo which migrated here from afar. Today this region is the granary of Canada. Summer wheat requires a growing season of 100 days over 10°C (50°F), which cannot be achieved if harvested after August 20th and is not at all possible in the north (limit of cereals). Barley needs 90 days and so can be grown further north.

The decreasing temperatures and increasing precipitation recorded by the climatic stations in Edmonton and Winnipeg mark the boundary with the boreal snow forest climate. In this region there are projecting tongues and islands of arable land where the cultivation of cereals has advanced.

Between the Great Lakes and St Lawrence River (Ottawa climate station)

In the corner between the Great Lakes and St Lawrence River lies Canada's most southerly region. The Great Lakes have a mitigating influence on temperature. The winter temperatures are higher than in the Prairies, the daily fluctuations somewhat less, the growing period reaches 160 days. Precipitation is evenly spread throughout the year; the weather is changeable owing to the areas of low pressure converging in the Great Lakes region and being "revitalised".

The following statistics illustrate the temperature increase from Ottawa in the direction of Detroit: annual mean temperature of Ottawa 5.7°C (42°F) (Detroit 9.9°C (50°F)), average July temperature in Ottawa 20.7°C (69°F) (Detroit 23.3°C (74°F)), average temperature fluctuation in January in Ottawa from −16 to +16°C (3 to 61°F) (Detroit −7°C to −0.6°C (19 to 30°F)). In the opposite direction towards the north-east of Ottawa the temperatures fall: annual mean temperature in Québec 4.4°C (40°F), average July temperature 19.3°C (67°F), mean temperature fluctuations in January from −16.7 to −7.7°C (2 to 18°F). The annual precipitation levels rise from Detroit (787 mm (31 in.)) to Ottawa (850 mm (33 in.)) and 1058 mm (47 in.) in Québec.

Canadian Atlantic provinces (Halifax climatic station)

The estuarine region of the St Lawrence River along with Novia Scotia and Newfoundland have a wet, temperate but cool climate. Northwards along the coast the temperatures fall, particularly in winter: annual mean temperature of Halifax 7.4°C (45°F), of St John's, Newfoundland 5.4°C (42°F); January average in Halifax −3.3°C (26°F), in St John's −6.9°C (20°F). The cause of this is the northern cold Labrador current which brings icebergs far south (up to 40°N; Titanic disaster). Fog is common in the sea area off Newfoundland as the mixing of the cold waters with the warm water of the Gulf Stream current results in the cooling of the air and condensation. Temperatures continue to fall northwards along the coast (compare Goose Bay climatic station).

Boreal snow forest climate (Goose Bay, Whitehorse climatic stations)

North of the climatic zones already described the growth period is too short for deciduous trees. This is the beginning of the boreal coniferous tree belt which extends monotonously and endlessly beyond Canada, around the northern hemisphere into Eurasia. Adequate warmth in summer (mean July temperatures over 12°C (54°F)) and low winter temperatures provide the ideal conditions for this type of forest in a broad belt right across the continent. There is a continental high centred between Hudson Bay and the Alaskan border with annual fluctuations in the monthly mean temperatures of over 40°C (104°F). In the interior the precipitation is low (Whitehorse 257 mm (10 in. per annum)), but owing to low evaporation and being in the form of snow, adequate for tree growth, unlike the southern Prairie regions.

In the regions where the temperature is not above 10°C (50°F) for more than 30 days (which corresponds to a July mean temperature of 12°C (54°F) the forest cannot survive and it gradually becomes tundra (barren grounds). This applies in eastern Labrador, near Goose Bay, in a narrow coastal strip quite far south, as the temperatures are suppressed by the Labrador current. Around Hudson Bay, the "icebox" of America, the tundra climate penetrates further south than anywhere else in the world on the same latitude (50°). Further inland north of the Great Slave Lake (Yellowknife climate station) the limit is much further north. The Great Slave Lake is frozen up to a depth of 2 m (7 ft), the Great Bear Lake 2.7 m (9 ft). Below the Great Slave Lake the River Mackenzie freezes over between November 17th and 30th until between May 1st and 14th when it thaws. Only heaths, mosses and possibly shrubs can thrive in the tundra climate. The limiting factor is the summer warmth and not the cold winters or low precipitation.

Polar Arctic climate (Yellowknife, Innuvik climate station)

Permafrost is present where the annual mean temperatures are below −7°C (19°F). This can reach depths of several hundred metres, limited only by the heat from the earth's core. On the surface it thaws in summer to a depth of 1.5 m (5 ft). As the meltwaters cannot seep away or evaporate at such low temperatures the ground is covered in bogs and water-logged, despite the low level of precipitation (below 250 mm (10 in.) per annum).

With annual mean temperatures down to −3°C (27°F) the permafrost only has vegetation in places. Coniferous trees can grow in the areas of

Formation of Icebergs

Course of glacier

Course of glacier

Course of glacier

Tongue of glacier

Iceberg

Atlantic Ocean

As it drops towards the sea large blocks of ice break off from the 'tongue' of the glacier; the glacier 'calves'; icebergs are formed and drift out into the open sea.

© *Baedeker*

summer thaw, the permafrost also occurs in the boreal snow forest. It can be recognised from the varied ground patterns; circles (on flat land) and stripes (on slopes).

Ice climate
(Isachsen climatic
station)

In the region of the numerous islands of the Canadian archipelago, the area around the magnetic North Pole, where average temperatures in July are below 6°C (42°F), there is no vegetation (average July temperature in Isachsen 3.7°C (37°F)) with the ground cover consisting of bare rock and scree. Although this Polar region is so easily flown over en route to Japan it remains inaccessible to the land traveller. It is a climate of extremes with either summer Polar days or winter Polar nights and only a short transition phase in between the two. As the climatic graph of Isachsen station shows the daily fluctuations in temperature are slight compared with the more southerly located stations, yet the annual temperature differences are great.

Pack ice, icebergs

The limit of the pack ice reaches the northern islands. The largest part of the Arctic Ocean is always frozen. The icebergs have jagged, irregular shapes. Mostly they have broken away from the Greenland glaciers. The surface of the sea also freezes causing floating ice.

Flora and Fauna

The flora and fauna are closely related to the geology, relief, soil conditions and climate. Roughly described Canada consists of 40 per cent treeless tundra and 40 per cent forest belt. Between the two is the zone of shrubs and small trees, known as forest-tundra. The grasslands with their fertile brown and black soils together with the mountain vegetation in the west and east make up a further 12 per cent.

Columbian pines

The boreal coniferous forest comprises about 82 per cent of Canada's forests, with the forests of the Cordilleras making up 9 per cent and the forest in the south-east a further 9 per cent. This dense zone extends 5000 km (3107 mi.) from east to west and is over 1000 km (621 mi.) wide. It is a region where summer temperatures (July) reach 10°C (50°F) to 17°C (63°F) and the mean January temperature does not drop below −30°C (−22°F). Precipitation only amounts to 350 mm (14 in.), but which is sufficient as there is little evaporation. Unlike northern Europe there are few pine trees but predominantly white and black spruce (*picea glauca, picea mariana*). In places tamarack (*larix laricina*) and in the east balsam fir (*abies balsamea*) occur. There is the occasional jack pine (pinus banksiana) in the south-east. The most common species of deciduous trees are birch (*betula*) and poplar (*populus*).

The spruce are of considerable dimensions. White spruce reach heights of 25 m (82 ft) with a diameter of 60 cm (24 in.), black spruce grow to 10–15m (33–50 ft) and have a diameter of 15–25 cm (6–10 in.).

Boreal coniferous forest

In the north forest and tundra merge with the boundary following the 10°C (50°F) July isotherm. This transitional zone is the habitat of the caribou. The herds graze on the open tundra in the summer, migrating over 1000 km (620 mi.) south in the autumn and returning north in the spring. They are continually pursued by packs of wolves which ensure natural selection takes place.

Forest-tundra

In the south the boreal forest belt becomes the park belt where only smaller wooded areas are found, mostly along the rivers. The park belt is the transition zone to the open grasslands. The most common tree is the trembling aspen (*populus tremuloides*) reaching a height of 10 m (33 ft) and a diameter of up to 40 cm (16 in.). Manitoba's lake region provides favourable habitat for bur oak (*querus macrocarpa*). Depending to their habitat they grow between 4–10 m (13–33 ft) high and 2–40 cm (1–16 in.) diameter.

Park belt

The soils of the boreal coniferous forests are generally heavily leached, consisting mainly of acidic podsoils which are unsuitable for agricultural cultivation. The grey-wooded soils are more fertile with some cultivation possible. More favourable soils may form on former glacial deposits.

Soils

Many different species of animals are to be found in the boreal coniferous forest. As well as the caribou and wolves already mentioned there are black and brown bears and deer, the most well known being the wapiti. This is also home to the bison. Smaller mammals include beaver, marten, foxes, muskrat and skunk. It is not surprising that trapping has been an important source of revenue for centuries and is still practised today.

Fauna of the boreal coniferous forest

The close relationship between the animal and plant kingdom is demonstrated by the beaver and beaver meadows which should therefore be examined in more detail.

Also much sought after for its fur the beaver (*castor canadiensis*) lives mainly in the water. When the water level is not high enough it builds dams from tree trunks, branches, stones and earth. Sometimes these dams can be up to 100 m (330 ft) long blocking the streams and forming 1–2 km (¾–1¼ mi.) long lakes which gradually fill up with sediment.

The build-up of water causes the forest to flood and die. This loss is much greater than that caused by the beaver to poplar, birch, alder and willow in its search for food. Having exhausted its food supply the beaver is forced to move on. The result is the destruction of the dam at the next high water. The reservoir overflows and "beaver meadows" form with luxuriant grass providing ideal pasture for elk, deer and buffalo which therefore remain for a long time.

Beaver

Canadian beaver

Beaver meadows are widely dispersed. Before the arrival of the Europeans the number of beaver was estimated at more than 10 million. Around 1800 hundreds of thousands of furs were exported from Québec alone. Over 200 dams were counted along a six mile long river and elsewhere about 70 beaver ponds in a 2 square mile area. The beaver meadows were also important for the first settlers. Land could be ploughed and hay produced and the woodcutters could find food for their animals. This short description illustrates the long-term effect that the beaver has had on Canada's original countryside.

Upland forests

The upland forests of the Cordilleras, which comprise 9 per cent of the total forest area, are more varied and sturdier, because of the terrain, than the monotonous forests of the boreal coniferous zone. The Cordillera can be subdivided into four regions: the sub-Alpine region, the montane region, the Columbia forest and the coastal region.

Sub-Alpine forest

The sub-Alpine forest covers the largest area. It extends along the eastern slopes of the Rocky Mountains, the slopes of the coastal ranges and along the edges of the interior plateaux. Spruce, fir and pine grow here, among them the engelmann spruce (*pica engelmanni*) which can reach heights of 60 m (196 ft) and a trunk diameter of 1.8 m (6 ft). Other important species of the sub-Alpine region include alpine fir (*abies lasiocarpa*) and lodgepole pine (*pinus contorta*). The firs and pines grow up to 30 m (98 ft) with a trunk diameter of 80 cm (31 in.).

Montane forest

The montane forest region includes primarily the interior high plains and is made up of pine, poplar and douglas fir. Dense pine woods (*pinus ponderosa*) are especially widespread, often the result of large forest fires whereby the seeds fall from the opened cones. In the more southerly river valleys of the montane region steppe grass and plants are an indication of the aridity.

In contrast the Columbia forest region around the Kootenay, Fraser and Thompson Rivers receives considerably higher levels of precipitation and has different species of trees. Western hemlock (*tsuga heterophylla*) and western red cedar (*thuja plicata*) are widespread.

In British Columbia 60 per cent of the land is wooded and only 1 per cent cultivated. Only the alluvial soils found in the river valleys are suitable for cultivation.

Columbia forest

The coastal region is characterised by particularly high precipitation and luxuriant plant growth. There is also a wide variety of species with a predominance of hemlock fir, cedar and douglas fir and especially sitka spruce (*picea sitchensis*). Spruce, fir, poplar, oak, maple and alder are also in evidence. The four most important types, hemlock and douglas fir, sitka spruce and cedar, are the major timber producers reaching heights of 50 m (164 ft) along the coast, with douglas fir even 100 m (330 ft), and trunk diameter of 4–5 m (13–16 ft).

Coastal region

The upland forests are the habitat of many animals. Hunting is, however, strictly controlled by the Wildlife Act. Big game include wapiti deer, elk, wild sheep and mountain goats as well as numerous mammals prized for their fur and predators such as black and grizzly bears.

There are many different species of birds and fishes, of which salmon and trout are the most common.

Fauna of the coastal range

Salmon up to 1.5 m (5 ft) long and weighing 35 kg climb up to the upper reaches of many rivers on their journey from the sea to their spawning grounds, where they each lay up to 30,000 eggs in the gravelly river bed. Many of them then die of exhaustion. The young salmon stay in the freshwater for up to five years before returning to the sea.

Salmon

Salmon going upstream to the breeding grounds

Flora and Fauna

South-east
Canada

The diverse species of mixed woodland make up the remaining 9 per cent of forest and can be divided into three regions owing to the mild, wet climate: the belt around the Great Lakes and St Lawrence River, the extreme south of Ontario between Lake Erie and Lake Ontario, the Acadian woodlands that surround the southern Atlantic provinces.

In this region the conifers are mainly red spruce (*picea rubens*), eastern hemlock (*tsuga canadensis*) and pines. The deciduous trees comprise birch, oak, beech, elm, aspen and maple. The red maple (*acer rubrum*) and sugar maple (*acer saccharum*) enjoy particular importance. The maple trees grow over 30 m (98 ft) tall and have a diameter of 60 to 90 cm (24 to 35 in.). Their hard wood is prized for the manufacture of furniture and the sap produces maple sugar and syrup.

For several species of tree the summer-green deciduous forests of southern Ontario are their northernmost limit. These include lime, walnut, hickory, oak, chestnut, tulip, magnolia, jasmine and sassafra, the softwood of which contains a heavily scented oil. The variety of species in this region is most apparent in September and October, when the "Indian Summer" reveals the colourful make up of the forest. This area attracts many tourists in autumn who come to see the rich colours of the foliage.

The varying proportion of woodland is interesting; in southern Ontario and on Prince Edward Island it is about 15 per cent, in northern Ontario about 90 per cent, in Nova Scotia 75 per cent and in New Brunswick 85 per cent.

Soils

The soil formation is patchy and varies between sands and loams. It consists mostly of podsols, which near the Atlantic are often rich in debris and difficult to cultivate. Narrow enclosed areas of arable land with favourable soil conditions are found in the St John River Valley and Annapolis Valley.

Grass steppes
(prairies)

The grass steppes and the park belt which surrounds them are only one third of the area of the neighbouring forest but are of great economic importance. Unlike the forest belt the natural vegetation has been completely displaced by cultivation. Old descriptions of the countryside make it possible to imagine how it was prior to 1870. Vast grasslands, which were easy to clear and fertile soils, created favourable conditions for farming from the start.

Tall grass

The tall grass, true grass prairie covers a relatively small area around the former Lake Agassiz, a former glacial lake. Grasses (*stipa spartea*) grow in dense formation up to 2 m (6 ft) high. Copses of elm trees (*ulmus americana*) are only found along the rivers.

Mixed grass

The flora of the mixed grass prairie is varied, with stipa and festuga being the prevalent grass species. The grass is less than 1 m (3 ft) and there is the occasional copse of trees which continue into the park belt or north into the forest belt.

Short grass

Many xerophilous plants are found in the short grass prairie, among them opuntia polycantha. As much of the land is used for grazing, owing to the low precipitation (6–7 arid months), many species of grass have been preserved. Woodlands are scattered in the Cypress Hills, which reach 1470 m (4822 ft) and tower 675 m (2214 ft) above the surrounding area.

Soils

The fertility of the prairies lies in the soils. They were heavily glaciated and are made up of up to 70 per cent medium grain, of which 15 per cent is sand or clay. Finer sands are located near former glacial lakes. They range from brown, through dark brown to black soils (*chernozems*). The proportion of cultivated land falls between 40 and 80 per cent, depending on the type of soil.

The animal world has undergone great changes in the Prairies. This used to be the home of the buffalo or bison, that migrated in great herds north in spring and south with the snowfall in the autumn. In the forest belt these migrations extend as far as the Great Slave Lake. Prior to European settlement the buffalo numbers were estimated at 60 million, with about 40 million left by 1830. By 1900 this magnificent beast had almost been wiped out with only 1000 left at the turn of the century. The virtual extermination of the buffalo had disastrous consequences for the Prairie Indians whose way of life was dependent on buffalo hunting. Efforts have been made to reintroduce and distribute these animals, requiring much patience and hard work. The numbers of antelope (*antilocapra americana*) were also much higher. Prairie dogs and numerous rodents are also found in the steppes.

Fauna of the grass steppes

The third type of vegetation in Canada, after the forest belt and the grasslands, is the tundra zone, which the visitor coming to Canada flies over for hours. Even from the air it presents a chilly and monotonous picture, justifying its name, the "barren grounds". This description, however, is not competely true as it is carpeted with colourful flowers for a few short weeks in summer before they die off.

Tundra

The vegetation of the tundra zone is exposed to extreme climatic conditions. Summer only lasts three months and biting and sharp winds prevail in winter as well as being extremely dry. The above climatic factors and the permafrost hamper soil formation with bare rock being common. Regosols are widespread with underlying tundra soils.

Climatic conditions

The range of vegetation is narrow and limited to lichens and reindeer moss, with occasional dwarf heathers and ericacae. Larger areas of vegetation are situated on the warmer southern slopes. In general the vegetation thins out from north to south.

Flora

A seal, ideally suited to the Arctic

Conservation

Fauna in the
tundra

The extreme Arctic conditions also affect the habitat of the animal kingdom. Large herds of caribou move twice a year between the tundra and
the forest belt usually covering 1300 km (over 800 mi.). The caribou is
essential to the Indian way of life, providing both food and clothing. It
also provides some variety in the diet of the Innuit who live mainly on
fish.

Unfortunately the caribou herds have been decimated in the last
decades, from 2.5 million in 1938 their numbers had declined to 800,000
in 1970. This drop is due to hunting with modern rifles. Packs of wolves
are also responsible for killing herds of caribou; a wolf kills an average
of 16 caribou during its lifetime. Road construction and forest fires have
also affected the caribou population.

The largest animals of the north are the musk-ox, found on the Arctic
islands where they feed on the sparse vegetation. Their numbers also
decreased dramatically until a hunting ban in 1917 stabilised the
population so that there are about 15,000 today. Unlike the caribou the
musk-ox only wanders over a limited area.

Wolves, Arctic foxes, Arctic hares, lemmings and squirrels (which
hibernate for eight months) are common. Their white colouring camou-
flages them with their surroundings. There are 80 species of bird which
prefer to nest around the Mackenzie delta. Around Baffin Island and
Southampton Island the indigenous Innuit hunt seals and polar bears.

Conservation

Canada is not a "land of unlimited opportunies", therefore it is essential
to conserve resources and protect the environment. The destruction of
the balance of nature began with the displacement of the long-established
lifestyles of the natives and continued with the slaughter of the buffalo
herds – whose numbers fell between 1831 and 1900 from 60,000,000 to
1000 – and the decimation of the caribou and increase in forest fires.

Soil erosion

In the farming areas soil erosion and dust storms reduce crop yields so
attempts are made to increase yields by "dry farming" (the ground is
regularly worked but not tilled every year) and "strip farming"
(100–200 m (330–660 ft) wide strips of land are interspersed with cereals
or left fallow). In eastern Canada overworked soils resulted in widespread
desert-like conditions, whereas excessive modernisation and rationalis-
ation has led to a reduction in the number of farms in the Prairies.

Over-fishing,
seal-hunting

Canada's unilateral decision to extend its fishing limits to 200 miles
(from 1977) attracted international criticism. The violence often associated with seal-hunting also provoked worldwide outrage.

De-afforestation

The timber industry, which used to provide timber for the construction
industry and fuel, today specialises in paper and cellulose production,
with the result that because of the low growth intensity of the trees the
new growth is not always ensured. Thus in many places further exploitation is only possible after 100 years.

Another disadvantage is that in Canada wholesale felling is the norm,
unlike the selective felling in Europe. This causes severe soil erosion
particularly in upland areas with high precipitation. Granting consent to
set up logging camps with high levels of production therefore has
environmental implications.

River pollution
Acid rain

Other problems are water pollution by the cellulose industry and
damage to the forests by acid rain. To put a stop to this danger the harmful emissions must be stopped at source. In Sudbury, a prime example
of environmental destruction because of its iron and nickel mining, a
360 m (1182 ft) high giant chimney stack, the highest in the world, has
been built. Pollution in the immediate vicinity of the town has certainly

The dramatic effects of acid rain

been reduced but in north Québec and Labrador, 1000–1500 km (620–930 mi.) away, acid rain has been detected which has adverse effects on the vegetation, soil systems, water quality, etc. Acid snow is also harmful with Schefferville having 48 per cent of its annual precipitation in the form of snow. Toxins collect in the snow cover during the winter causing high levels of acidity after the snowmelt.

The degree of the air pollution can be measured from the emissions, which were originally 3600t per day, later reduced to 2200t and now down to 700t. Sudbury is only one of many places producing emissions, others are in northern Québec and southern Ontario (Hamilton).

However, the Canadian polluters are overshadowed by the giant industrial concerns in the United States (Chicago-Gary, Indianapolis, Pittsburg, etc.).

The detrimental effects of acid rain on the fishing and forestry industries and the recreational value of the Great Lakes have been the subject of negotiations which have been taking place for years with the USA and are keenly followed by the population living around the Great Lakes. Reduction of coal-burning to lower air pollution is the main issue.

Other agreements between the neighbouring countries concern the Great Lakes, near which no less than 40 million people live, which together with the concentration of industry creates great problems. Canada's ability to influence the agenda is, however, weakened by the fact that a large proportion of its industry is dependent on US capital. Further subjects of conflict are the transcontinental and sub-Arctic pipelines and roads. The Mackenzie Pipeline and Dempster Highway have altered the paths of the caribou and weakened the native economy to the extent that the very existence of the inhabitants is threatened.

Extensive open-cast mining, slag heaps and difficult access routes are the conflict areas created by the mining industry. The huge mining areas of the oil sands in north Alberta present problems of world importance.

Mining

Conservation

At St James Bay and at other gigantic hydro-electric power stations the land treaties with the Indians were infringed resulting in delays lasting years and even decades.

A particular problem is presented by the off-shore oil-fields off the coast of Newfoundland. These oil rigs lie in the path of the cold Labrador current, which causes hundreds of icebergs to drift annually south from Greenland. A collision would have disastrous environmental consequences as some of the world's most important fishing grounds are located here. A surveillance and warning system operates with tugboats guiding the icebergs away from a collision course.

National parks

In order to minimise the above problems the Department of the Environment was established in 1971 in Canada, earlier than in other countries, and was given responsibility for national parks in 1979. The first signs of a change of direction were at the end of the 19th c. when the national parks in Canada were founded in conjunction with the development of the transcontinental railways and following the national park idea in the USA (Yellowstone Park was founded in 1872).

In contrast to the popularly held opinion that in Canada conservation would be more strictly implemented than in the neighbouring USA, as far as the national parks are concerned, the opposite is true: legislation is less forceful. The impression is given that tourism is valued more highly than actual conservation. In the well known parks of the Canadian Rocky Mountains whole towns have grown up, and on the Athabasca glacier it is considered advisable to use powerful snowmobiles.

In 1885 an area of 25 sq. km (10 sq. mi.) was placed under protection on the east slope of the Rocky Mountains. The idea behind the national parks was to provide recreation and pleasure for people at the same time educating them to respect nature. Development is restricted to visitors' centres, pathways, camping and picnic sites with restrictions on exhibitions, hotels, petrol stations and shops.

The first seven parks were established between 1885 and 1914 in the Cordilleras. They are Banff (opened 1885; 6641 sq. km (2563 sq. mi.) at present), Yoho (opened 1886; 1313 sq. km (507 sq. mi.)) and Jasper (opened 1907; 10,878 sq. km (4199 sq. mi.)) on the vertex of the Canadian Pacific Railway and Canadian National Railway (formerly "Canadian Northern") in the Rocky Mountains, as well as Waterton Lakes National Park (opened 1895; 526 sq. km (203 sq. mi.)) which is connected with the US Glacier National Park, Mount Revelstoke Park (opened 1914; 263 sq. km (102 sq. mi.)) in the Selkirk Mountains. Away from the Cordilleras are Elk Island Park, founded before 1920, (194 sq. km (75 sq. mi.)) east of Edmonton and the smaller national parks St Lawrence Islands (4 sq. km (1½ sq. mi.)) and Pointe Pelée (16 sq. km (6 sq. mi.)) in Ontario.

Since 1920 national parks have been opened in nearly all regions of Canada. In the Cordilleras these were Kootenay Park (1378 sq. km (532 sq. mi.)) and the Pacific Rim Park (389 sq. km (150 sq. mi.)), along with the huge Kluane National Park (22,015 sq. km (8498 sq. mi.)) with Canada's highest mountains (Mount Logan, 5951 m (19,531 ft); Mount St Elias, 5489 m (18,015 ft); Mount Lucrania 5226 m (17,152 ft)) and the Northern Yukon National Park (6050 sq. km (2335 sq. mi.)).

In the sub-Arctic and Polar north there are no fewer than five national parks of enormous areas such as Wood Buffalo Park (44,807 sq. km (17,296 sq. mi.)), Ellesmere Island Park (39,500 sq. km (15,247 sq. mi.)) and Baffin Island Park (21,471 sq. km (8288 sq. mi.)). Today there are 32 national parks distributed over all provinces and territories. The majority are situated in the Cordilleras (6), the Northwest Territories (5) and on the Atlantic coast (9).

Monuments, historic parks

In addition to the national parks there are another 63 national historic parks, of which 42 alone are to be found in the Atlantic provinces and in the St Lawrence Lowland. For example, they include Louisburg and

Annapolis Royal in Nova Scotia or Upper Canada Village in Ontario. For the planning of future national parks Canada has been divided into 39 natural regions each with different geological and morphological structures and ecosystems.

Apart from the 32 national parks at present there are about 1200 provincial parks totalling 300,000 sq. km (115,800 sq. mi.). Whereas the national parks come under central government jurisdiction the provincial parks come under control of the provinces. These are more equipped for larger crowds of visitors and often have sport and recreational facilities. Popular provincial parks include the Laurentides in Québec, the Cypress Hills and the Dinosaur Park in Alberta. All nature parks referred to have an increasing importance for tourism.

Provincial parks

Population

In area Canada is the second largest country in the world after Russia, but in terms of its population it is in 33rd place. According to the 1997 census there were approximately 30.3 million people living in Canada. The population density of about 3 inhabitants per sq. km compares with 227 per sq. km in Great Britain.

In Canada the vast expanses of the north are almost uninhabited compared with the relatively uninterrupted densely populated narrow strip along the border with the USA. The "empty spaces" in the north – Yukon and Northwest Territories – with their severe weather conditions and poor soils are only inhabited by 0.3 per cent of the population.

Regions

Province/territory	1961		1997	
	population	%	population	%
Newfoundland	457,853	2.5	563,600	1.9
Prince Edward Island	104,629	0.6	137,200	0.5
Nova Scotia	737,007	4.0	948,000	3.1
New Brunswick	597,936	3.3	762,000	2.5
Québec	5,259,211	28.8	7,420,000	24.5
Ontario	6,236,092	34.2	11,408,000	37.7
Manitoba	921,686	5.1	1,145,200	3.8
Saskatchewan	925,181	5.1	1,023,500	3.4
Alberta	1,331,944	7.3	2,847,000	9.4
British Columbia	1,629,082	8.9	3,933,300	13.0
Yukon	14,628	0.1	31,600	0.1
Northwest Territories	22,998	0.1	67,500	0.2
Canada total	18,238,247		30,286,900	

About 62 per cent of the population live in Québec and Ontario, where the population density in the south of the provinces along the St Lawrence River and north of Lake Erie and Lake Ontario is 66 per sq. km. This is the highest concentration of population in the country. A mild climate, good soils and favourable communications have contributed to the economic development of this region. The land to the west is relatively thiny populated owing to the unfavourable physical conditions – the rocky substratum of the Canadian Shield produces poor agricultural soils. The fertile wheat-growing area of the prairie is heavily populated to the west of Winnipeg.

There a few clusters of population in the upland areas of the Cordilleras with higher concentrations around Vancouver and along the

Population

Edmonton-Calgary axis. The increasing popularity of this region can be attributed to its cosmopolitan attitudes and beautiful countryside. Unlike the east it does not have the burden of historical tradition and is more cosmopolitan. Instead of fighting against each other, ethnic groups have worked together here to create a new society inspired by the pioneering spirit.

City-country

Since the end of the Twenties, relatively late in comparison with Europe, the population has been chiefly urban. Reasons for this were the later onset of industrialisation and the importance of agriculture especially in the Prairies. In recent years there has been an increase in the rural population. This has not taken place among the farm workers, on the contrary, their numbers have declined. It is caused by the increase in areas in relative proximity to the cities. Ecological reasons and lower prices along with well developed communications are responsible for people leaving the cities. Urban lifestyles and working patterns are thus transferred to the outskirts of conurbations.

Development

The demographic changes are dependent on two factors: the natural increase in population (births less number of deaths) and the net immigration (immigration less emigration).

In the period 1986–94 the population increased by 8 per cent – still a particularly high rate of increase for an industrialised country. Well over half this increase was accounted for by natural growth.

The baby boom of the Fifties was followed by a drastic fall in the birth rate in the Sixties, generally attributed to the contraceptive pill but also because of people marrying at a later age, economic prosperity, social security and other factors. Even in Catholic Québec, where the birth rate was always higher than in other provinces, population growth has been low in recent years.

The mortality rate is 7/1000. Increasing life expectancy – 80 for women and 73 for men – has resulted in an increase in the number of old people in the population. The proportion of those under 15 fell to 19 per cent in 1997, in 1961 it was 34 per cent. Those over 65 increased from 8 per cent to 13 per cent in 1997.

Immigration

Canada is still a country where immigration takes place. In 1994 immigrants made up one sixth of the population. From the historical point of view immigration is a key factor in the population development of this country. It went in cycles and was dependent on economic processes. At the beginning of the century and after the Second World War immigration was particularly high running parallel with economic upturn. Having over a long period stabilised at 120,000 per annum, recent years have seen a dramatic increase in the level of immigration, with an estimated inflow in 1997 of 226,000.

Previously immigration policy was subject to frequent revision. At times restrictions were placed on the numbers of Chinese and Japanese, preference being given to applicants from Britain, Ireland, America and France. Nowadays these distinctions have been lifted in favour of a greater ethnic mix. During the Sixties and Seventies there was a shift in the proportion of Europeans and Asians: in 1975 40 per cent of immigrants still came from Europe and 25 per cent from Asia, in 1980 the proportion of Asians was up to 50 per cent. With the obligation to take refugees and keep families together the preference was for well educated workers. The immigrants settled mainly in the conurbations around Toronto, Montréal and Vancouver; in 1997 over half of all immigrants were living here.

Migration

In recent years there has been an increase in migration to British Columbia. There is a more even balance of population in the west although the main areas of population are still in the central provinces.

According to the 1991 census 1 million people belong to the original population: 4 per cent of the total population. Among this group are 50,000 Inuit and 784,000 Indians. The remainder are mixed race, including 213,000 Métis – descendants of Indians and French. In addition there are large numbers of Canadians who have given up their status as Indians. Most of the original inhabitants live in the north and west. In the Northwest Territories they comprise almost two thirds of the total population, in the Yukon Territory about a quarter, in Manitoba and Saskatchewan a tenth, but only 1 per cent on Prince Edward Island. The forebears of these peoples or "First Nations" as they call themselves, came to Canada from northern Asia over the Bering land bridge or via Greenland on the edge of the Polar ice cap.

This group of the population is the only one not to have prospered through the economic development of the country. Following the arrival of the white man the number of Indians was heavily decimated by wars, expulsion and the introduction of diseases. For two hundred years contact between them consisted chiefly of fur trading. Skins and furs were exchanged for weapons, etc. The Indians became socially and economically dependent.

In adapting to the modern world they gave up a way of life that was perfectly in harmony with the land to copy the white man's way of life. Unemployment is twice as high as it is among the immigrants; the average income is between ½ and ⅔ that of the rest of the population. Moving to the cities frequently brings the well known problems of alcoholism and crime; crime rates are between three and five times higher than the national average.

Various measures have been introduced to combat the social disadvantage faced by the original inhabitants: special education programmes with teacher training for their own schools, air-lifted medical aid in remote areas, financial support and greater participation in decision-making through local government and involvement on political committees.

Ethnic groups (1986)	population	%
Single race	18,035,665	72.1
Mixed race	6,986,345	27.9
French	6,087,310	24.3
English	4,742,040	18.9
Scottish	865,450	3.5
Irish	699,685	2.8
German	896,715	3.6
Italian	709,585	2.8
Ukrainian	420,210	1.7
North American Indian	286,230	1.1
Dutch	351,765	1.4
Chinese	360,320	1.4
Scandinavian	159,335	0.6
Jewish	245,860	1.0
Polish	222,260	0.9
Total	25,022,010	

There are over 50 different Indian languages and dialects which belong to ten linguistic groups: in order of importance they are Algonquin (60 per cent), Athabasca, Iroki, Salish, Wakasha, Tsimischian, Sioux, Kutenai, Haida and Tlingit. 70 per cent of registered Indians live in reservations on their own land. Nearly every Indian belongs to one of the 576 so-called bands, administrative and political units with their own property and historic associations.

The reservations which were allotted to the Indians by the Europeans are only of limited economic potential. They are usually handicapped by

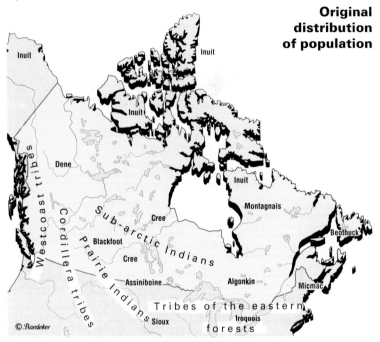

Original distribution of population

Inuit

Inuit

Inuit

Inuit

Dene

Inuit

Westcoast tribes

Cordillera tribes

Sub-arctic Indians

Prairie Indians

Montagnais

Cree

Blackfoot

Beothuck

Cree

Assiniboine

Algonkin

Micmac

Tribes of the eastern forests

Sioux

Iroquois

© Baedeker

a peripheral location, poor communications and infrastructure. Most of them have developed a basic subsistence economy. Those with minerals or forestry reserves or else are in locations with tourist appeal are the exceptions. Although the Indians were not dealt with as ruthlessly in Canada as in the USA there are still countless incidences of unfair treaties. A recent conflict occurred in Montréal in 1991 with plans to turn land which was regarded as sacred by the resident Indians into a golf course.

Inuit

The word "Inuit" means "person", whereas "eskimo" means "eater of raw meat" in the language of the Algonquin Indians. The latter term is not used by the Inuit themselves but rather regarded as discriminatory. Altogether there are about 100,000 Inuit in the Arctic regions of the world, i.e. Greenland, Alaska, Russia and Canada. Their language is called Inuktitut. Seven different groups can be distinguished on the basis of economic and cultural practices: the Mackenzie, the Copper, the Netselik, the Caribou, the Iglulik, the Baffinland and Labrador Inuit. These are not tribes; the Inuit did not have tribes as such. Historically three cultures have been identified: the Pre-Dorset culture (2500–800 BC), the Dorset culture (up to 1300 AD) and the Thule culture (up to 1750). The Inuit live in small communities on the Mackenzie delta, on the Arctic islands and on the mainland coasts of the Northwest Territories, in Labrador, on Hudson Bay and the Ungava Bay. Their location on river estuaries, fiords and in other coastal areas reflects their original economic activity – fishing.

The classical picture of their life – canoe trips, living in an igloo, fishing at a hole in the ice, walking on snowshoes and hunting caribou with sledges pulled by dogs – belongs to the past. The modern world has

An Indian of the forests *An Inuit girl*

arrived even here with all its comforts and complications: aeroplanes (not many settlements are without a runway), snowmobiles, motor boats, permanent houses with every possible kind of technology from video to refrigerator (strangely necessary as the milk flown in from the south has a limited shelf life and the hole in the ice is no longer fashionable as a means of storage). The houses are prefabricated in the south and simply assembled here. Apart from fishing, employment is found in the extraction of oil, gas and minerals. The interests of the Inuit are represented by various organisations – the Inuit Tapirisat of Canada or the Inuit Development Corporations; two Inuit have seats in the Senate.

Mother tongue (1991; selection)	population	%
English	16,170,000	60.0
French	6,503,000	24.1
Italian	511,000	1.9
Chinese	499,000	1.8
German	466,000	1.7
Indo-Iranian	301,000	1.1
Chinese	212,000	0.8
Polish	190,000	0.7
Ukrainian	187,000	0.7
Spanish	177,000	0.7
Indian/Inuit	173,000	0.6
Dutch	139,000	0.5
Greek	126,000	0.5
Arabic	108,000	0.4
Hungarian	80,000	0.3

In Canada there are 80 ethnic groups with almost as many different languages, of which the founder nations Great Britain (40 per cent) and France (27 per cent) plus inhabitants of English or French descent make up over 80 per cent. A long way behind are the Germans (2 per cent), followed by the Italians (2 per cent), who came after the Second World War, then the Ukrainians with 1 per cent. The number of Russian and East Europeans has increased following the opening of the borders in the early 1990s and the collapse of the former Soviet Union.

In recent years there has been a particularly marked influx from Asia, especially Chinese from the south-east Asian region, including the former British Crown colony of Hong Kong, but also from India, Pakistan and Iran. Today more than 2 per cent of the population have Chinese as their mother-tongue. Other ethnic groups have also increased. These tend to be English- rather than French-speaking. 60 per cent of the population have English as their mother tongue, 24 per cent French, the remaining 15 per cent other languages. The ethnic composition is rather more heterogenous than the linguistic structure.

Those of French descent are concentrated around Québec, where about 80 per cent of the population have French as their mother tongue. The rest of the Francophone population live in the neighbouring regions of New Brunswick and Ontario. In the upper classes of some cities an affected form of old-fashioned English is deliberately cultivated. More than 80 per cent of the economic elite belong to families which came from Great Britain. However, 15 years under the French Canadian prime minister Pierre Trudeau contributed to breaking down the traditional hierarchy of nationalities.

In 1977 French became the only official language in Québec – for which the Separatists had fought hard and has caused much resentment. Not only in schools and government but also in business French has become important. Québec has formed a linguistic enclave, as it were.

16 per cent of the population speak English and French. This bilingual group lives primarily in south Ontario and south Québec and at the so-called Soo-Moncton-Line separates both the main language areas. According to the Constitution Act 1982 both languages have the same status, rights and privileges in all parliamentary and government institutions. Both language areas have been reinforced; instead of the sought-after bilingualism there is separation. Cultural dualism brings problems as well as enrichment.

This is the in-word of the last two decades, although the idea has been around for much longer. Canada is not so much of a melting-pot, as, for example, the ideology of the United States was represented until recently. It is more a kaleidoscope of nations who preserved many of their characteristic ethnic features. There is even a ministry for multicultural affairs. It is a question of maintaining people's links with their homelands through preserving manners and customs in clubs and through the media as well as promoting cultural pluralism and intercultural communication.

Religion

The dominant religion in Québec was Roman Catholicism, influencing politics and society, whereas Anglican Protestantism was prevalent in the other provinces. Traditional religious and ethical values were promoted and the rural conservative society was protected from change.

It was not until after the Second World War that religious pluralism developed with the new wave of immigrants. Mennonites and Hutterer settled mainly in the Prairie states, Jews were more at home in the big cities, Japanese Buddhists in the west and Buddhists from south-east

Menonnites in Ontario

Asia in Toronto, Hindus and Sikhs in the conurbations. Para-religious groups are growing in influence.

Today the three most important religious groups are the Roman Catholic church, the United Church of Canada and the Anglicans. Next in importance are the Presbyterians, Lutherans and Baptists.

The religious communities create a very vivid picture because of their history of colonisation. They are influential in many spheres on account of their socio-economic structures, their different lifestyles, their mentality and marriage lines, and also their international associations.

Religious communities

In addition to the numerous communities there are numerous sects with between 5000 and 30,000 members, of which the most important are the Nazarenes, Dukoborzen, Hutterer, Moravian Brothers and Unitarians. In 1981 245,000 people were members of the numerous other Protestant splinter groups. A total of 1,788,995 people did not belong to any religious group, though only 4455 described themselves as atheists.

Several churches and sects are even further fragmented making the overall picture even more colourful. This is the case among the Anglicans, Presbyterians, Baptists as well as the Reformed and Orthodox churches which have different relationships with their mother church and even celebrate their festivals according to different calendars.

According to the 1981 census Christian denominations are in the majority in keeping with the European background of the Canadian population.

Among the Christian population there are three main groups, the Catholics with just 50 per cent, the Protestants with over 40 per cent and the Orthodox with 2 per cent of the faithful.

The largest Protestant religious communities in Canada are the United Church (almost 4 million members), the Anglicans (2.5 million members), the Presbyterians (about 800,000), the Lutherans (about 700,000), the Baptists (around 70,000) and the Pentecostalists (about 350,000).

There are interesting regional differences between the denominations reflecting the ethnic backgrounds. The French dominated provinces of Québec and New Brunswick have with 90 per cent and 50 per cent respectively the highest percentage of Catholics, all other provinces have a Protestant majority, but throughout all provinces and territories (with the exception of British Columbia) the Catholic church is the strongest religious community. It is less dominant in the Prairie provinces.

In Newfoundland, Québec and both territories the Anglicans are the dominant branch of the Protestant church, in the other provinces it is the United Church. The Catholic church has more members in the provinces of Québec (5.6 million) and Ontario (3 million), the United Church of Canada in Ontario (1.7 million), British Columbia (600,000) and Alberta (550,000), the Anglican church in Ontario (1.2 million), British Columbia (400,000) and Alberta (200,000), the Presbyterians in Ontario (500,000 followers) and British Columbia (100,000 followers) and the Lutherans in Ontario (260,000 followers), Alberta (150,000 followers) and British Columbia (130,000 followers).

Even on a communal basis there are regional differences. All communes of the province of Québec have a Catholic population of more than 50 per cent, often more than 90 per cent. The same applies to communes in New Brunswick, on Prince Edward Island, in Nova Scotia and in south-west Newfoundland, as well as towns in northern Ontario (provincial average 30 per cent) and north Saskatchewan. In various parts of Newfoundland, northern Ontario, Manitoba and northern Alberta Catholicism is still in first place but only includes 25 to 50 per cent of the population.

In almost all other areas the United Church of Canada is in top position. It reaches over 50 per cent in some parts of southern and western Ontario and Manitoba, in almost all the remaining towns in southern Ontario, the south of the Prairie provinces and in British Columbia it lies between 25 and 50 per cent.

The Anglican church of Canada represents between 25 and 50 per cent of Vancouver Island and the sparsely inhabited regions of Yukon Territory, Labrador and Newfoundland (up to 50 per cent here in places!). Baptists are found in the south of Nova Scotia and New Brunswick. Apart from the main denominations mentioned above the Mennonites in south Manitoba surpass 50 per cent.

In second place are the United Church of Canada in Manitoba and Saskatchewan (each with between 25 and 40 per cent) and the Ukrainian Catholics and Greek Orthodox in Manitoba (10 to 40 per cent), together with the Mormons in southern Alberta. The situation is most simple in Québec province, most complicated in the Prairie provinces where as many as six different religious communities are significantly represented.

Many Protestant communities feel more closely involved with each other than with their mother churches in Europe. This explains how the Methodists, Congregationalists and Presbyterians came together to form the United Church of Canada in 1925.

Non-Christian communities also are found in certain regions. Half of the Jewish population live in Ontario, with a further third in Québec, where they make up 2 per cent of the population.

The distribution of those not belonging to any religious group forms an interesting pattern. It is at its lowest in Newfoundland comprising 1 per cent and in Nova Scotia 4 per cent, average in Ontario and Manitoba with 7 per cent and numbering 12 per cent in Alberta, 20 per cent in the Yukon Territory and 21 per cent in British Columbia. Their numbers more or less doubled between 1971 and 1990.

The individual groups are all showing different patterns of development. Within the last ten years the Unitarians fell by 30 per cent, the Presbyterians by 6 per cent and the Anglicans by 3 per cent. On the other hand the United Church grew 1 per cent, the Jews almost 10 per cent and the Catholics by 13 per cent. Largest increases were among the Mormons with 36 per cent and the Pentecostalists with 54 per cent. The most significant increase of all, however, was among the Buddhists whose numbers rose by 223 per cent to 52,000.

Education and Science

The Canadian educational system is equally as diverse as its multi-cultural society. Education is highly regarded at national and provincial level.

Education is in second place after social security on the scale of govern-ment responsibilities. Funding of education is derived from 7 per cent of Canada's gross national product and 8 per cent from private income. The major proportion of the education budget comes from county and municipal government.

Finance

Up until the end of the 1960s the Canadian education system experienced tremendous expansion through a constantly growing population and increasing economic capacity. Huge universities were built and new courses introduced to meet the demands created by the rise in student numbers. By the beginning of the Seventies this period seemed to be at an end with the falling birth rate. This wave spilt over into the entire education system but underwent further growth in the middle of the Seventies. The Eighties are characterised more by stagnation in the educational sphere as demographic trends and a reduction in economic capacity indicate.

Development

Following the amalgamation of the four former provinces in 1867 edu-cation became the responsibility of the provinces. The Canadian consti-tution does not recognise (since 1981/82) federal control over the education system. The state is only responsible for marginal groups which do not come under the jurisdiction of the provinces: original settlers, personnel and relatives of the Canadian armed forces and offenders in penal institutions are subject to federal authority. The state, however, has indirect influence over financial transactions concerning provincial educational policy, especially where further education, direct funding for employees or support for bilingual education is involved.

Federal presence

While the provincial education departments are legally associated with the state, the day-to-day activities of public (i.e. state) schools are the responsibility of the regional administrative bodies, which are com-posed of elected and/or appointed representatives. The commune is responsible for school buildings, transport, employment of teachers and for setting the local taxes to maintain the schools.

All pupils have to attend basic school; different schools have the same curriculum. Pupils of the Junior High schools can choose some of their subjects. The colleges are not only institutions which prepare pupils for university, they also offer vocational courses. The Canadian school system incorporates various types of schools: private schools, denomi-national schools and further education colleges.

Basic schools

The private schools are an alternative to the state schools. They nor-mally have a religious, linguistic, social or academic bias. The extent to which a provincial government supports such schools depends upon the individual province.

Private schools

There are denominational schools in five of Canada's provinces. Traditionally Newfoundland's state schools are controlled by ecclesiasti-

Denominational schools

cal Roman Catholic religious groups which are subdivided into school areas. The main Protestant groups (Anglicans, United Church, Salvation Army) founded their schools and administration in the mid-Sixties. Even the Pentecostalists and the Adventists maintain schools. Québec has a dual school system: one for Roman Catholics and one for non-Catholics.

Ontario, Saskatchewan and Alberta have a majority of Catholic schools, with fewer Protestant schools.

Further education	For many years the only form of further education was at university. Now there are further education and technical colleges in all provinces.
University-type institutions	Canada has several institutions which award university degrees: There are colleges where study in various disciplines can lead to a doctorate, or institutes of art, religion and theology as well as engineering and education colleges. Military academies also feature among the tertiary institutions. Admission to university is conditional on having completed prescribed courses and having studied at an appropriate high school.
Community colleges	The "Community Colleges" are an alternative to university which are distributed throughout all the Canadian provinces; there are specialist schools for art, science, technology, agriculture and fishing, marine and paramedical technology, even nurses are trained here. Applicants must have successfully completed a course of study at a secondary school.
Business and technology schools	Business and technology are essentially covered by public and private schools of business and commerce, courses in specialist schools and related institutions.
Adult education	Adult education in Canada enjoys particular regard. These courses are financially supported by trade unions, communal organisations, churches, public libraries, government departments, trade and industry. The courses can lead to recognised qualifications or they can just be taken for personal interest.
Universities	About ½ million students are matriculated at Canada's 70-odd scientific universities with an equally sizable teaching body. The leading universities are in Montréal (Université de Montréal, McGill University), in Toronto (University of Toronto), in Edmonton (University of Alberta) and Québec (Université de Québec).
Research	Canada's rich supply of minerals, the absolutely immense, sustainable resources (forest, cereals) and the enormous potential of hydro-electric power have greatly inspired science and research. Thousands of scientists are employed in mining, energy, electronics, forestry, transport and communications. During the last two decades great achievements were made in the area of news transmission (e.g. construction of news satellites), data transmission and communication, long-range reconnaissance and geophysical exploration. Advances have also been made in medical research, especially in the field of laser surgery, radiology and remote-control dentistry. Pioneers in medical research are the university clinics in Montréal and Toronto. Canadian research in the areas of plant and animal breeding, pest control and soil science has achieved international recognition. It is not without reason that Canada exports wheat and other vegetable and animal products to the value of 6 billion dollars per annum. More recent subjects of Canadian technological research are nuclear energy and transport systems. Canada is in the forefront of the aeroplane construction and space industries. Considerable success has also been achieved in researching new forms of energy and energy conservation.

Canadian researchers are at the forefront of environmental research. Since 1986 they have been using fluorescence line imagers (FLIs) which measure chlorophyll fluorescence. Using this equipment the growth of algae in seas and lakes or even damage to forests caused by acid rain or other environmentally harmful factors can be measured. This equipment has already been used successfully in the Black Forest in Germany. Other projects are being planned or else about to be put into operation, partly in connection with the European Space Agency (ESA).

The Canadian "Natural Science & Engineering Council" is responsible for, promotes and supervises research projects. This involves exchanges between scientists of similar associated institutions abroad and the organisation of scientific congresses and meetings.

Government

Canada is a federation of states with a parliamentary monarchy consisting of ten provinces and two territories. The capital is Ottawa.
The national flag is the "Maple Leaf". Since 1980 it has had its own national anthem and in 1982 the first Canadian constitution, the Canadian Act, replaced the British North America Act of 1867. The British parliament is no longer responsible for Canadian parliamentary affairs.

The head of state is the British Queen Elizabeth II. She is represented by a governor general, recommended by the Canadian cabinet and appointed by her. Apart from representative duties and signing laws he officiates at the appointment or dismissal of ministers or at the dissolution of parliament.

The executive power is shared between the prime minister and the cabinet, which is accountable to the lower chamber and whose members are also usually members of parliament. Should the lower chamber withdraw its confidence in the prime minister then he must resign from office and elections take place. The prime minister also can call a general election during his five year period of office.

The legislative power is shared between the governor general, the senate (upper chamber) and the "House of Commons" (lower chamber).
The upper chamber consists of 104 senators from the provinces and territories, who are appointed by the governor general on the recommendation of the prime minister. It is the lower chamber of 282 delegates elected by a first-past-the-post system which is decisive in the legislative process: it is responsible to the prime minister and only here can financial laws be introduced. In general both chambers have an equal say in legislative matters. For its part the senate can simply delay the final passing of laws.

The Canadian constitution does not recognise the existence of parties. An exception is the "Election Expenses Act". Yet parties do exist within the framework of the parliamentary monarchy. The "National Liberal Federation of Canada" emphasises social security and foreign and economic independence, while the "New Democratic Party", a member of the Socialist Internationale, represents moderate socialism. The "Parti Québecois" exists only in Canada and represents the movement for autonomy in this province. Also there is the "Social Credit Party", found mainly in Alberta and British Columbia, the "Progressive Conservative Party of Canada", which supports membership of NATO and the Commonwealth and the preservation of the present economic system, and the Creditists (protagonists of social credit) representing the underprivileged classes.

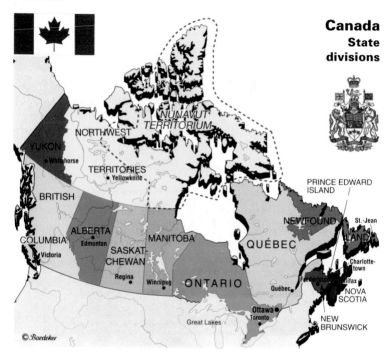

Canada
**State
divisions**

| Provinces and territories | Canada is made up of ten provinces and three territorial regions. The provinces have their own constitution and their governmental procedures are more or less identical to that of central government. Central government is represented by a provincial governor who is appointed for five years by the governor general on the recommendation of the prime minister. The provinces have their own legislative bodies with the exception of the Supreme Federal Courts. Legislative authority is not categorically defined; state and province compete with each other in this area. It is the responsibility of the province to raise its own taxes, to pass laws relating to civil rights or communal administration and to organise social welfare. The provinces also have control over the health service, education and use of natural resources. The administration of the Yukon Territory, the Northwest Territories and Nunavut is directly accountable to the federal government but is becoming increasingly independent. |

Courts

Administration of the courts lies with the provinces, apart from matters which concern the Supreme Federal Court. The Canadian laws are laid down in the "Common Law". Québec has its own civil laws based on the French "Code Civil". The highest courts in Canada are the Supreme Court and the Federal Court in Ottawa.

The judges of the federal and provincial courts are appointed by the relevant federal or provincial parliament. Canadian justice is thereby independent of the legislature and executive.

Armed forces

Conscription does not exist in Canada. Volunteers must serve at least five years. The total size of the army is about 90,000 men. Basic and specialised training courses are run by signals command and the

Royal Canadian Mounted Police on Parade

Canadian Forces Training System. In 1968 formal divisions between the army, air force and navy ceased to exist.

The British North American Act of 1867 gave the provinces the right to form their own police authorities.

Police

In 1873 the Royal Canadian Mounted Police (RCMP) came into existence. The function of these "redshirts" was not only to keep law and order but also to see that federal laws were observed. Nowadays about a 20,000-strong force operates in the sparsely populated regions of the country. They are found in eight provinces and the two territories which come under the jurisdiction of the federal government.

RCMP

Financially better off provinces such as Québec and Ontario as well as individual regions and towns maintain their own police forces ("Sûrté", "Security").

The Security Service, which controls the secret service, complements the activities of the RCMP in protecting public property and important personalities.

Security Service

Québec Problem (see Baedeker Special p. 398)

The national unity of Canada is most threatened by the situation in Québec, the francophone region of the country.

The cause is rooted in the historical tug-of-war between the British and French Canadians which began when the British took over New France in 1763.

Origin

On the one hand the influence of the French Canadians in social and economic areas was severely restricted. The consequences were that, forced by the process of economic development, these areas became dominated by the British Canadians: they occupied the key positions, whereas the French Canadians had no part in decision-making and their average income was far below that of the British Canadians. This disparity existed until quite recently.

On the other hand, however, the French-speaking inhabitants of Canada set about gradually populating the areas which were exclusively settled by the British Canadians. An easy undertaking, for these regions were insecure land for the anglophone population on account of the USA bordering in the east and the French Canadian region situated in the west.

"Silent revolution"

In 1960 the Liberal party got into provincial parliament with the French Canadian candidate Jean Lesage. This signalled a turning-point in history known as the "silent revolution". It was Lesage who forcefully demanded independence for the francophones and succeeded in not only getting the federal government to tolerate the struggle for cultural independence but also to set up a commission to solve the problem of bilingualism and twin culturalism. The result was the recognition throughout the country of French as the second official and equal language alongside English.

"Saturday of the rubber truncheons"

The independence movement did not always run so smoothly. Not long after the election of Lesage the FLQ (Front de Libération de Québec), a freedom front, was formed which sought attention through terrorist attacks, demonstrations, revolts, acts of spying and bomb attacks.

The political tension came to a head in 1964 with the visit of the British queen. The consequence of these disturbances was the start of the migration of English-speaking population from this province; this caused the loss of the business directors with their entire management staff and left Québec in an ecomonic impasse.

Nationalism

When General de Gaulle publicly proclaimed his demand for a free Québec in 1967 the vehement defenders of separatism and the withdrawal of Québec from the Canadian federation regarded themselves as completely justified: the nationalist wing of the Liberals split from the party and founded the "Parti Québecois". They made a breakthrough in 1976 when René Levesques became the new president of Québec. However, they lost in a referendum in 1980 which was to have been the basis for negotiations on sovereignity within the confederation; 60 per cent of the population of the province of Québec voted against it. Since then serious efforts have been made to make Québec more French. Another referendum was defeated in 1995.

Law 101

In 1977 the famous Law 101 was passed which made Québec a monolingual francophone province with considerable restrictions on the use of other languages. The "Office de la Langue francaise" (Office of the French language) has since set about systematically changing everything to French.

English expressions which are used and recognised worldwide, advertising, names of companies and street names have all been translated into French. A "hot-dog" is referred to as a "chien-chaud".

Collapse of traditional order

Not only has there been a reduction in the British Canadian population in this province through migration as a consequence of Law 101. The traditional order, centred on the church, collapsed. Indicative of this is the abrupt decline in the birth rate since 1960; it is the lowest in Canada, whereas the traditional francophone family structure reflects a particularly high birth rate. 1960 is also the year when migration of French Canadians from the country to the towns began. In the province of Québec four out of five inhabitants live in urban conurbations.

The cultural identity also altered. Today they are proud of their heavily accented language, "québecois"; there is a French Canadian literary movement independent from France and its literary classics, which also influences music and art.

Nowadays French Canadian politicians hold office in nearly all government departments.

The separatist movement of Québec is not just an isolated problem within the Canadian confederation. Other provinces such as Alberta, British Columbia and Newfoundland are seeking to break away from the federation.

Québec is merely the most visible example of one of Canada's basic problems.

Economy

There are only a few countries in the world where a summary of the economy contains such a high number of superlatives as for Canada. One of the richest countries in the world and, at 9.97 million sq. km (3.85 million sq. mi.), second only to Russia in area, in 1997 it ranked 33rd among the world's economies, with a population of 30.3 million and gross national product per head of 20,167 $. Its economic structure has been shaped for years by productive agriculture and the extraction and processing of its own raw materials. Canada is one of the largest producers of wheat and barley and possesses enormous forests (2.5 million sq. km (1 million sq. mi.)) which supply the giant cellulose and paper industries. It is a leading producer of uranium and zinc ores. Not least Canada has massive supplies of energy, especially gas and oil, as well as ideal conditions for producing hydro-electric power. Together with other factors this contributed to Canada having the highest rate of energy consumption in the world (about 9700 kg (21388 lb) oil units per head in 1992) and the lowest energy prices of all industrial nations.

The advantages and disadvantages of the geographical conditions in this northern country are reflected both in its geomorphological features and surface features (natural vegetation and soils) and in the climatic difficulties of distinct regions. Exploitation of the diverse range of natural resources is often problematic and can only be overcome by employing the most modern technology and involving considerable investment. The climate, in particular, exerts a lasting influence on the agriculture, mining and transport. Climate and permafrost do not only hinder treefelling and mining in the north, but also – through snowfalls and blizzards – the centres of population in the south of Canada. Examples of the natural favourable and unfavourable conditions and their effects on the economic suitablility or exploitation are: mineral wealth of the Canadian Shield and the Cordilleras, abundant oil reserves in the Interior Plains stretching north, the giant forests of the boreal coniferous zone in the north and the mountains in the west (Cordillera) and east (Appalachians), the former grass steppes of the Prairies or the St Lawrence Valley as the fertile site of one of the most important granaries in the world, finally, the Atlantic and Pacific coastal regions and the inland lakes as fishing grounds and the waterfalls in the mountains and of the Canadian Shield, which provide hydro-electric power at an increasing ecological cost.

Following the discovery of Canada by the Europeans, in the first instance Jacques Cartier, who sailed up the St Lawrence River in 1534, colonisation began which continued into the 20th c. Canada's original population of about 200,000 Indians and Inuits in the 16th c. were equally as unable to defend themselves as those of the USA, but the massacres and wars did not take place to the same extent. Influential in the early economic development were four staple goods: fish, animal skins, wood

ALBERTA
WHEAT POOL
FARMER OWNED
CO-OPERATIVE
ATHABASCA
POOL
ALBERTA
WHEAT POOL
ATHABASCA
Canada
Government of Canada
Gouvernement du Canada

and cereals. From the beginning of the 17th to the middle of the 19th c. fur-trading was organised by the powerful Hudson's Bay Company with economic proceeds being less relevant than exploration of the country by hunters, traders and surveyors. The widespread takeover of the fur trade by the increasingly prosperous wood trade was caused by the value of wood as building material for the British fleet and also more and more for settlements and companies at home. Settlement was quickly followed by cultivation and at the beginning of this century 60–70 per cent of the Prairies were turned over to wheat, with Canada being the prime exporter of wheat. The discovery of mineral wealth in the middle of last century combined with the parallel opening up of the country by the railways gave the economy further support which brought industrialisation to the doorsteps of the exploding American markets and determined typical attitudes and outlook for a long time.

The period of development that follows is very similar to that of many European countries and if this is omitted and the present day political economy examined then it can be seen that on the one hand Canada has thrown off its old image and has remarkable high technology capable of competing on international markets, on the other hand, in accord with the US economy, it has been in recession since 1990 and is confronted by debt mountains, empty cash desks and unemployment, as never known before in the country.

Mulroney era

The development of the Canadian economy has always been closely linked with political challenges. From the founding of the dominion in 1867 with the British North America Act the situation was characterised by the breaking away from England. When despite granting extensive cultural sovereignity the new constitution in 1982 failed to integrate the francophone province of Québec, a growing uncertainty arose from the complex situation. Although Brian Mulroney, leader of the government, still had a clear majority in parliament with 159 seats out of 295, surveys showed increasing support among voters for the Liberals and Social Democrats. Out of the close economic relationship with the USA, accompanied by heated discussions in Canada, the free trade agreement came into operation on January 1st, 1989, which foresaw the dismantling of all reciprocal trade restrictions. The national debt exceeded the 400 billion Can.$ mark in mid-1991, with annual interest of 43 billion Can.$ or 6.2 per cent of the gross national product in the current financial year. High mortgage rates and overpriced consumer credit caused bankruptcies from 1989 to 1990 to rise by 44 per cent and disturbed the high living standards of the Canadians, which were financed by budget deficits. Not until 1993 did economic growth rise above 2 per cent; even then, while inflation fell below the 3 per cent mark, the unemployment rate that same year reached a historic high of 11.3 per cent.

Chrétien era

The North American Free Trade Agreement (NAFTA), signed by the governments of Canada, the USA and Mexico which came into force on January 1st 1994, created the largest internal market in the world, with a total population of 365 million and an annual economic output of some 6 billion US dollars. The Chrétien government promised a much needed boost for Canadian industry, particularly in the fields of telecommunications, computer software, space and aeronautics, agriculture and forestry, environmental conservation technology and mining. Since then – i.e. in 1998 – unemployment has fallen to 8.4 per cent.

Agriculture

On account of geographical conditions the most productive agricultural area is concentrated in a 300 km (186 mi.)-wide strip along the border with the USA. Employing almost 500,000, in 1996 this corresponded to 3.3 per cent of the working population in almost 280,000 farms (average farm size more than 200 ha), agriculture and forestry produced 3.3 per

◀ *"Cathedrals of the Prairie" and a silo train*

cent of the gross national product in 1996. In the same year agricultural exports amounted to 8 per cent, forestry products 12 per cent. In total about 8.6 per cent of the land is used for agriculture. Different type of farms are found in different regions.

The large cereal farms dominate the three Prairie provinces (Manitoba, Saskatchewan and Alberta), where about 50 per cent of the agricultural income is generated on about 80 per cent of the land thereby forming the backbone of agriculture.

Dairy farms are found mostly in Québec, Ontario and Nova Scotia, cattle rearing farms in Alberta and Ontario and specialised crop farms (vegetables, fruit, tobacco, potatoes and ginseng) in every province.

In 1996 Canada's main crops were beef, milk and milk products, pork, poultry and eggs, wheat, rape seed, barley, maize, rye, soya beans, potatoes, vegetables and fruit.

The high productivity results from intense mechanisation and the degree of specialisation on the farms. A predominance of almost exclusively family concerns is a further guarantee of responsible accounting and profitability. High productivity has, however, also necessitated a corresponding level of capital investment and an increase in debt. Therefore it is not surprising that even in Canada the number of farms is decreasing and farming is increasingly concentrated in the hands of the top giant concerns.

Fishing

Canada is one of the leading fish exporters in the world. From annual catches of 1 mill. tonnes about a third is exported, 66 per cent to the USA. Lucrative fishing grounds are situated off the Atlantic coast, especially for cod, plaice, mussels and lobster. Herring and salmon are caught off the Pacific coast. On account of the drop in the fishing quotas in the Seventies Canada decided to expand its fishing zone to 200 miles and to restrict the quotas for the north-west Atlantic in its negotiations with the EU. The crisis of the Atlantic fishing industry with factory closures and further reductions in quotas is exacerbated by the overfishing of the North Atlantic by the large Spanish and Portuguese fishing fleets. By 1993 the situation had deteriorated to such an extent that a total ban had to be imposed on fishing in the waters around Newfoundland. Several thousand Canadian fishermen and workers in ancillary industries lost their jobs as a result.

Fur trade

In the early phase of economic development the trade in furs was of great importance and a trade mark of the Canadian economy. Worldwide protests against the fur hunters (especially against the cruel seal hunting), the introduction of fur farming and the general fall in demand have led to the downturn of this branch of the economy and at best it is a specialised market.

Forestry

Forestry is one of the mainstays of the Canadian economy. Every year some 150 million cu. m (5,298 million cu. ft) of timber are felled, mostly for processing by the paper and cellulose industries or for use in building. Annual production of cellulose is well over 12 million tonnes, of paper and cardboard in excess of 15 million tonnes. Several hundred thousand jobs are thus directly or indirectly dependent on forestry.

The timber industry, however, has for years been the focus of critical debate. 'Clear cutting" and insensitive reafforestation schemes continue to generate a bad press. A "Green Plan" was initiated to carry out re-afforestation, but the secondary forest, predominantly high-yielding spruce monoculture, is susceptible to insect attack and winter storm damage. Nor does it reproduce the ecosystem of the original forest.

Today the country is united in its determination to introduce environmentally sustainable forestry, including reafforestation. More than 1700 km (656 sq. mi.) of trees are now being planted every year.

Hitherto production at Canada's numerous cellulose, paper and cardboard factories has involved the use of vast quantities of chlorine bleach, afterwards released, usually untreated, into rivers and lakes. Now this environmentally very damaging chemical is being replaced by less harmful alternatives.

Canada has the richest and most productive deposits of minerals and fossil fuels in the world. More than three dozen different minerals are mined in large quantities including iron, gold, copper, silver, nickel, lead and zinc, also uranium, cobalt, cadmium, molybdenum, titanium and platinum. Less well known metals are also extracted as by-products of larger operations. Canada is the global leader in the production of several minerals. It is also one of the world's major producers and exporters of fossil fuels (natural gas, oil and coal).

Mining

The vulnerability of Canada's mining industry to political factors is well illustrated by the case of uranium, extraction of which has been substantially reduced in recent years as a result of falling demand. Not only are fewer nuclear power stations being built, but military requirements have also decreased dramatically with the ending of the Cold War, The resultant overproduction and collapse of uranium prices has put the existence and profitability of some mines in doubt.

At the start of the 1990s mining accounted for about 5 per cent of Canada's gross national product. Falling world commodity prices, expanding recycling initiatives and substitute materials, reduced demand in key industries such as the construction and automobile industries, special factors (uranium) and the cost imposed by a hostile environment (climate) have caused output to fall in many sectors of the industry.

In 1996 Canada produced around 550 billion kWh of electricity, the 4th highest output globally. Of this, about 70 per cent was hydro-electricity, an exceptionally high percentage by international standards. The largest hydro-electric power stations in the world are to be found in the provinces of Québec and Newfoundland. The generating giant Hydro-Québec (annual turnover in excess of 5 billion barrels), has a major stake in the massive St James Bay project which should eventually produce many tens of thousands of megawatts of electricity. The benefits of such huge projects are today being increasingly questioned however, not only by Conservationists but also by government.

Energy

Although Canada is proud of its oil reserves (ca. 5 billion barrels), recent years have seen a restructuring of fossil fuel production away from oil into natural gas. In 1990, as a result of the Gulf crisis, Canadian energy producers enjoyed high export returns; in autumn 1998 prices were lower.

The dependence of Canadian industry on the country's own agricultural and mineral resources is reflected in the structuring of the processing industries. In 1995 this sector of the economy accounted for about a fifth of gross national product and 16 per cent of employment. The major industrial centres are in the big conurbations of Montréal, Toronto, Winnipeg, Calgary, Edmonton and Vancouver. The majority of jobs are in the automotive industry, Ford Motors of Canada, General Motors of Canada and Bombardier being the most important companies by far.

Industry, trade and services

Food and associated industries come next, with 200,000 employees, The growth of industries producing capital goods has been stimulated since the mid 1960s by tax allowances enjoyed by the American automobile industry in return for greater investment.

Additionally, though not without interruption, the Mulroney government's liberal economic policy "promoted" direct foreign investment, which was channelled towards the service sector and increased dependence on the US economy. Between 1970 and 1990 alone, private sector employment rose by 7 per cent (to 33 per cent). It is now estimated that three out of four jobs are in commerce, transport and the service industries.

Economy

In 1988 the head offices of fifteen of Canada's 20 largest companies, as well as banks, insurance companies and other service providers, were located in Montréal or Toronto. Over the last decade, however, cities such as Edmonton, Calgary and Vancouver have emerged as major regional centres, The province of Alberta has experienced a sharp upswing owing to the boom in oil and natural gas and in the construction industry,

Foreign trade

In 1995 the value of goods exported amounted to some 219 billion US$, about a fifth going to the United States and much smaller proportions to Japan (4 per cent), Great Britain, South Korea and Germany (1 per cent each). The main categories of exports were vehicles (25 per cent), machinery and technical equipment (23 per cent), manufactured goods (18 per cent), forestry products (9 per cent) and consumer items (3 per cent). The export of high-tech products alone accounted for 30 billion US$.

In the same year Canada imported goods to a value of 201 billion US$, about a third being machinery and equipment, a quarter vehicles, and a fifth other manufactured products. The main sources of imports were the USA (about 66 per cent), Japan (5 per cent) and Mexico (3 per cent).

Thus in 1995 Canada had a balance of trade surplus of 17 billion US$. It hardly needs emphasising that Canada has a particularly close economic relationship with the USA.

Tourism

Tourism has advanced dramatically as a sector of the economy. In 1996 income from tourism reached 6.6 billion US$. Of the more than 17 million foreign visitors to Canada, nine out of ten were from the neighbouring United States, underlining the importance of excursions, shopping and business trips between the two.

Even so, the high expectations formed by the Canadian tourist industry in the 1980s, and in particular the rapidly expanding hotel and catering sectors, remain largely unfulfilled except at local level following intensive promotion.

Overview

Throughout the 1980s and early 1990s the Canadian economy appeared trapped in a seemingly interminable "vale of darkness", the outward manifestations of which were a massive burden of national debt and a huge budget deficit. Since 1993 however there have been signs of recovery. In the third quarter of 1993 the rate of economic growth reached 3.9 per cent for the first time in many years, reflecting on the one hand increased consumer spending and on the other a particularly buoyant export performance. Within a year exports rose 15.6 per cent. In 1995 there was a surplus on the balance of trade of 17 billion US$. Growth of 2.4 per cent is forecast for 1999.

The creation in 1998 alone of 449,000 new jobs is indicative of the current buoyant state of the Canadian economy. At the end of 1998 the unemployment rate was just 8 per cent.

Giving less cause for optimism however is the exceptionally high level of national debt, which in the financial year 1994/95 reached a record 891 billion Can.$. Economic barriers between the provinces, relatively high wage costs and the expensive network of social provision are further factors affecting the economy. Also of concern is the continuing high rate of youth unemployment which at the beginning of 1999 stood at 14.5 per cent.

Outlook

In conclusion the following problem areas exist from an economic point of view:

reduction in the disparity between east and west and the difference between central and peripheral development (for example Alberta with the establishment of growth industries on the outskirts);

solving the conflict between development and conservation (further opening up of the north);

defusing idea of cultural dualism as a threat but as a source of enrichment instead (Québec problem);

format of relations with the USA, Mexico and the EU;

conservation of the unique natural environment (co-ordination and consolidation of the environmental laws, reinforcement of conservation measures, national parks).

Transport and Telecommunications

In the huge country of Canada, whose population is traditionally very mobile, a well organised transport and communication network must be guaranteed. This is particularly the case in view of the fact that Canada belongs to the leading industrial nations of the world. Owing to its sheer size it is imperative for the development of the Canadian economy and to maintain a high standard of living that well developed transport facilities and routes and the most up-to-date communication systems are available.

The technical problems presented in building an effective transport and communications infrastructure have motivated numerous Canadian entrepreneurs, scientists and engineers to great achievements. The innovative skills of Canadian technicians are in demand wherever there are problems with telecommunications, pipeline and road construction over rough terrain and civil aviation.

Shipping is of paramount importance to this huge North American country. A large percentage of export goods (especially ores, building material, wood and cereals) are transported by ship. The St Lawrence Seaway was widened to allow regular maritime harbours to be built on the Great Lakes in the middle of the country and along the St Lawrence River. Thunder Bay on Lake Superior is one of the main ports for the export of cereals. Huge quantities of minerals are exported from Sept Îles/Pointe Noire and Port Cartier (all in Québec province). On the other hand the ports of Québec (town), Montréal, Toronto and Hamilton are important for the import of oil products, coal, vehicles, etc. Situated out on the Atlantic coast are other major ports (Halifax in Nova Scotia, St John in New Brunswick, and St John's in Newfoundland) and on the Pacific coast (Vancouver in British Columbia). In the Pacific port of Vancouver alone more than 64 million tonnes of goods are handled annually.

Shipping

Alongside the continually expanding volume of freight traffic passenger services also operate, but on a smaller scale. The ferry services around Inside Passage (from Vancouver to Alaska) and among the Atlantic Islands in the east (especially Prince Edward Island, Newfoundland, New Brunswick, Nova Scotia) are of regional importance.

The main destinations of cruise ships are Vancouver and the Inside Passage, the Atlantic port of Halifax and the ports of Québec (town) and Montréal on the St Lawrence River.

Passenger services

The major Canadian railway companies, "Canadian National" (CN) and "Canadian Pacific" (CP), maintain a network of almost 100,000 km (62,139 mi.) of track. The railway lines of the east–west routes (on some routes north–south) are primarily used to transport freight. Extra long goods trains with 100 and more wagons, often pulled by up to six locomotives, move the freight between the cereal producing areas or ore deposits and the nearest sea ports and in return distribute the goods imported through these ports. There is considerable rail freight crossing over into the USA and vice versa.

Railways

Passenger rail services are provided by the company "VIA" Rail, founded in 1978. It rents the infrastructure from the major railway

Passenger trains

61

Transport and Telecommunications

companies and is concentrated on profitable lines with large numbers of passengers (e.g. the "racetrack" Toronto–Montréal) and tourist routes. In areas where passenger numbers are low provincial authorities or large companies fund passenger services (e.g. Ontario Northern or the Algoma Railway) for politically environmental reasons.

Roads

As in the neighbouring USA the motor car controls everyday life in Canada. The road and motorway network is particularly well developed in the heavily populated south and in tourist areas. At the end of the Eighties there were almost 450 cars to every 1000 people! There are 1 million kilometres (about 600,000 miles) of long distance roads which are used not only by tourists, but predominantly by whole caravans of gigantic trucks. At 7871 km (4890 mi.) long the TransCanada Highway is the longest road in the world connecting St John's on the Atlantic with Vancouver on the Pacific.

Snowmobile

In the long, harsh Canadian winters the importance of the caterpillar snowmobile cannot be underestimated. In the far north whole snow trains (trucks on caterpillars) are formed to make a path through the snow. In winter some of the frozen rivers function as roads. On the Mackenzie in particular and northern rivers this transport is common.

Air transport

Passenger air traffic is important because of the distances and morphology of the country. The main International airports are at Toronto, Montréal, Edmonton, Vancouver, Calgary, Winnipeg and Halifax.

Regional transport

Numerous larger and smaller airline companies operate from the above Canadian airports (almost 600 altogether). They serve the less populated regions and the far north, which is being opened up. These airlines use mostly smaller planes which can operate from the difficult runways on the 200 or more airfields.

Tele- communications

Canada, the home of Alexander Bell, possesses the most intensive telephone network in the world. For every 100 inhabitants there are nearly 53 connections. The Canadian telephone companies maintain the largest microwave transmission system in the world, which is capable of not only transmitting telephone conversations but also radio and television programmes and electronic data.

Recent applications include surgical operations in hospitals in other cities being monitored and assisted by remote transmission. Similar monitoring can take place in prospecting for raw materials and for land and sea travel guided by satellite.

History

Archaeological discoveries indicate that the predecessors of the present day Indians and Inuits were hunter-gatherers who filtered in over the Beringia land bridge in three waves from the north-east Asia to North America: first the predecessors of the northwest coast Indians, then the Inuit and finally the Paleo Indians.	*c.* 15,000 to 12,000 BC
Beginning of settlement in south Ontario.	*c.* 10,000 BC
The west coast Indians' culture flourishes.	*c.* 4000 BC
The Inuit populate the northern regions of Canada.	*c.* 3000 BC
Irish monks are said to have landed in the Gulf of St Lawrence.	*c.* 875 AD
Vikings stop temporarily in Newfoundland and Labrador. They build a short-lived township, evidence of which exists at L'Anse-aux-Meadows.	*c.* 1000
Portuguese, English, Normans and Bretons come to the rich fishing grounds of Newfoundland.	14th c.
John Cabot – probably born Giovanni Caboto in 1449 in Genoa and later entered the service of the English crown – reaches the eastern tip of Canada. He claims the country for England (Henry VII). Cabot contributes to the opening up the northwest Atlantic fishing grounds.	1497
Spanish, Portuguese and French fish off Newfoundland.	Early 16th c.
Verrazano reconnoitres present day Nova Scotia for the king of France.	1523
The Breton Jacques Cartier lands in Newfoundland after a long sea journey. He sails up the St Lawrence River to the Indian settlement Hochelaga (Montréal today). He opens the way into the interior for French colonists and fur hunters.	1534
Frobisher looks for the Northwest Passage and claims his discoveries in the Canadian north for the English crown.	1576
The first Hugenots settle here.	1604
Samuel de Champlain founds the settlement of Québec. It becomes the first successful white settlement and main town of New France. Champlain builds up an extensive trading network (fur trade) and becomes the first governor of French Canada.	from 1608
Henry Hudson, on behalf of the Dutch East India Company, also searches for the Northwest Passage. He names the great inland lake in north-east Canada.	1609/1610
Jesuits arrive in Québec and begin missionary work among the Indians.	1625
French pioneers found Montréal. The Iroquis attack the settlement for 20 years.	1642
Louis XIV of France declares New France to be a royal province. Troops are dispatched to defend the colony and further colonisation by France is encouraged.	1663

History

from 1670	The Hudson's Bay Company is founded by royal charter in London in 1670. The English king Charles II awards the company the fur trading monopoly for 8 million sq. km (3 million sq. mi.) of land. The English controlled company competes with French traders for favour with the Indians. The French extend their sphere of influence west along the St Lawrence River to the Great Lakes and from there to the Prairies and to the Mississippi. The English move southwards down the North American east coast.
1672	Louis Jollet and Father Marquette reach Lake Michigan and probably the Mississipi.
17th c.	The French found numerous settlements along the St Lawrence River and in Acadia (area south-east of the mouth of the St Lawrence, nowadays Nova Scotia, New Brunswick, southern part of Québec). Acadia is ruled by the French and English at different times.
1690–1713	The French explorer Pierre de Vérendrye extends the French fur trading posts to Saskatchewan and Missouri.
1745–48	As a counterpart to the inheritance wars in Europe war breaks out again between the French and English in North America.
1755	Shortly before the outbreak of the Seven Years' War several thousand French settlers are expelled from Acadia by the English governor for not being prepared to swear an oath of allegiance to England.
1759/1760	The period of power struggles between France and England in North America ends with the defeat of Montréal and Québec by British troops.
1763	Following the Paris peace agreement all colonies become British. France only retains the islands of St Pierre and Miquelon off Newfoundland.
1770–72	Samuel Hearne, commissioned by the Hudson's Bay Company, undertakes expeditions into the interior in order to increase the opportunities for trade. He is the first white man to reach the Arctic Ocean.
1774	In the Québec Act England guarantees the Québecois, who far outnumber the British settlers, the right to the French language, French civil law and to practise Catholicism.
1775–83	In the American War of Independence, in which 13 British colonies break away from the motherland and form the United States of America, Canada retains its neutral loyalty to Great Britain. Many loyal to the Empire (about 40,000 to 60,000) move north at the end of the war and settle in Nova Scotia, New Brunswick and in southern Ontario. This immigration changes Canada from a French colony of England to a predominantly English-speaking country.
1778	The first Europeans, led by James Cook and George Vancouver, land on the coast of present day British Columbia.
1783	In the Paris peace treaty the USA–Canadian border is established.
1791	The British government passes the Canada Act (the name Canada appears officially for the first time), which divides the old province of Québec into Upper Canada (nowadays Québec province) and Lower Canada (nowadays Ontario province), mainly English-speaking.
1792	George Vancouver, who took part in the expedition along the Pacific coast with James Cook in 1778, sails round the island which today bears his name.

An overland expedition led by Alexander Mackenzie reaches the Pacific Ocean.	1793
On one of the biggest expeditions of all time Simon Fraser travels 1368 km along the river named after him, from its source in the Rocky Mountains to its estuary in the Pacific. He names the region west of the Rockies New Caledonia, after his homeland, Scotland.	1808
The United States of America attempts to assert its influence over Canada by force. It results in war with Great Britain which ends in defeat for America.	1812–14
Great Britain initiates a campaign among its poor population, particularly in Ireland and Scotland, to encourage them to emigrate to the North American colonies.	1823
After 1830 chiefly Irish, Scottish and Germans emigrate to Canada. Numbers are estimated at 800,000 for this period.	1830–50
Uprisings take place in Upper and Lower Canada in protest against the authoritarian government, but are quickly put down.	1837
Upper and Lower Canada are united in the British colony of Canada. They receive a governor, an executive council, and an elected lower chamber, in which both the former provinces are strongly represented.	1841
The 49th parallel becomes the border between the USA and the British colonies from Ontario to the Pacific coast.	1846
The British create the colony British Columbia, which is united with the separate colony of Vancouver Island in 1866.	1858
The present day provinces of Ontario, Québec, New Brunswick and Nova Scotia form the autonomous dominion of Canada.	1867
The huge northern and western territories, which until now have been administered by the Hudson's Bay Company, join the new state.	1869
The Métis (French Indians), under the leadership of Louis Riel, rebel against the Canadian government.	
The province of Manitoba is established.	1870
British Columbia joins the Canadian federation.	1871
Prince Edward Island also becomes part of Canada.	1873
Russian Mennonites settle in Manitoba.	1875
The Métis, led by Loius Riel, rebel again. Riel is hung. The transcontinental stretch of the Canadian Pacific Railway is completed.	1885
The Gold Rush erupts on the Klondike/Yukon. On account of the increased population the Yukon is made a separate province from the Northwest Territories.	1896
Canadian troops fight for the British in the Boer War.	1899–1902
Alberta, Saskatchewan and the Northwest Territories are recognised as Canadian territories.	1905
Canada joins the First World War on the side of England. It results in further industrialisation and in Canada earning new international status	1914–18

Search for gold in the Klondike

through being an independent signatory of the treaty of Versailles and as a member of the League of Nations.

1919–25	The most serious disturbances in Canadian industrial history: workers strike to support their demands for social justice. Even the farmers are dissatisfied with their financial situation.
1921	William Lyon Mackenzie King becomes prime minister. He determines Canadian politics for 27 years.
Early 20th c.	Millions of immigrants from the USA, the British Isles and many regions of continental Europe populate Canada. The two main waves of immigrants are during and after both world wars.
1929–33	The world economic crisis reaches Canada. In 1933 unemployment peaks at about 20 per cent.
1931	The statute of Westminster grants Canada full autonomy.
1939–45	Canada fights against Germany in the Second World War.
1942	The Alaska Highway to Alaska is completed.
1945	Canada becomes a member of the United Nations.
1949	Canada becomes a member of the North Atlantic Treaty Organisation (NATO). Newfoundland becomes the tenth province of the Canadian Federation.
1959	The St Lawrence Seaway, an American-Canadian project, is opened.

Parliament passes the first Bill of Rights. It gives the Indians and Inuit the right to vote in federal elections. — 1960

The red maple leaf becomes the national flag. — 1965

Canada celebrates its centenary. — 1967
Expo '67 takes place in Montréal.
On July 24th Charles de Gaulle calls out from the balcony of Montréal Town Hall "Vive le Québec libre!" (= Long live free Québec).

Pierre Trudeau becomes prime minister. — 1968
The Québecois party is founded. Its aim is a separate, francophone state of Québec.

Parliament passes the Official Languages Act, in which both English and French are recognised as official languages. — 1969

Revolutionaries from the Front de Libération de Québec (FLQ) kidnap a British diplomat and a Canadian minister. Pierre Trudeau declares martial law. — 1970

The Olympic Games take place in Montréal. — 1976

In a referendum about 60 per cent of the population of Québec reject separatism. The Province remains in the Canadian Federation. — 1980

Canada receives a new constitution and a "Charter of Rights and Freedoms", in which human rights are guaranteed. — 1982

Demonstrations take place throughout the country against the government's decision to allow American cruise missiles in Canada. They are unsuccessful. — 1983

Bilateral meetings between prime minister Brian Mulroney and Ronald Reagan. Main topics are acid rain and the expansion of trade between the two countries. In Vancouver Expo '86 is opened. — 1985/1986

Canada is the first country in the world to establish in law multiculturalism. — 1988
In the elections of November 21st the Progressive Conservative party achieves an overall victory, but loses its two-thirds majority. Brian Mulroney is re-elected prime minister.
Canada and its biggest trading partner, the USA, ratify a free trade agreement.
The Winter Olympics are held in and around Calgary.

At a conference of foreign ministers of NATO and the Warsaw Pact in Ottawa the four super powers together with both German states declare their support for German unity. — 1990
The Meech Lake Agreement, which grants Québec province special status, collapses partly owing to the Cree chiefs in the Manitoba parliament, who vote against granting the descendants of French immigrants special status. As a result the activities of the separatist movement in Québec increase.
In Oka and in Montréal militant Iroquois resist the extension of a golf course which would violate the cemetery of their ancestors. A policeman is killed in the disturbances. Canadian police are sent in against the Indians.
In the Indian reservation of St Regis (north-east of Lake Ontario) members of an Iroquois tribe fight each other. Supporters and opponents of an organised gambling game fight bitterly with weapons causing deaths.

History

<table>
<tr><td>1991</td><td>In the summer a strike by postal workers disrupts public life.
In the autumn discussions on the reform of Canada's constitution come to a head. Once again the main issue is the granting of special status to the francophone province of Québec.</td></tr>
<tr><td>1992</td><td>In the spring the native inhabitants of the Canadian north opt for the creation of a new province, to be carved out of the existing Northwest Territories.
A referendum organised by the federal government decides against a new Canadian constitution.</td></tr>
<tr><td>1992/1993</td><td>The majority of Canadian troops stationed in Germany are withdrawn, returning to their North American homeland.</td></tr>
<tr><td>1993</td><td>In May Prime Minister Brian Mulroney signs the Nunavut agreement in Iqaluit granting self-government to the native inhabitants of Canada in the approximately 2 million sq. km (772,000 sq. mi.) eastern section of the Northwest Territories, stretching from the North Pole to the southern Hudson Bay. In June Mulroney resigns after nine years in office; he is succeeded by Canada's first woman prime minister, Kim Campbell. In subsequent parliamentary elections in October the Liberal Party emerges the clear victor; the Québec separatists, the Bloc Québécois, also make gains, becoming the second most powerful opposition group. The Liberal leader Jean Chrétien takes over as prime minister.
Responding to the crisis in fish stocks resulting from over-fishing, the federal government bans fishing in the waters around Newfoundland. Several thousand fishermen and employees in the fish industry lose their jobs.
On the Pacific coast of Canada strong resistance develops to further destruction of the remaining, still largely virgin, temperate rain forest eco-systems, threatened by continuing expansion of the paper and cellulose industries.</td></tr>
<tr><td>1994</td><td>On January 1st the North American Free Trade Agreement (NAFTA), signed by Canada, the USA and Mexico, comes into force. With some 365 million inhabitants and annual economic output of approximately 6 billion US dollars, the NAFTA countries constitute the most viable internal market in the world. The Chrétien government launches a billion dollar programme aimed at reducing unemployment which has now reached double figures.
In September the provincial election in Québec is won by the separatist Parti Québécois.</td></tr>
<tr><td>1995</td><td>In a separatist-instigated referendum on October 30th the people of Québec vote by the narrowest of margins (about 50,000 votes) to remain part of Canada.</td></tr>
<tr><td>1996</td><td>Fuelled by favourable exchange rates, Canada experiences a tourist boom with large numbers of overseas visitors. Air Canada and the German airline Lufthansa forge a close business partnership.</td></tr>
<tr><td>1997</td><td>The longest road bridge in the western hemisphere is opened; 13 km (8 mi.) long, it spans the Northumberland Strait between New Brunswick and Prince Edward Island.</td></tr>
<tr><td>1998</td><td>In a referendum at the end of November the Nisga'a Indians of north-west British Columbia approve a settlement of their claims to land. About three quarters vote in favour of what is described as a "historic" agreement.</td></tr>
<tr><td>1999</td><td>On April 1st Nunavut (Inuit for "Our Land") becomes an independent territory, split off from the former Northwest Territories. Nunavut law and the Nunavut land agreement guarantee Inuit living in the new territory self-government and the continuance of their traditions and heritage. Though the new territory is the largest of all the Canadian provinces and territories, this arctic region has a mere 25,000 inhabitants.</td></tr>
</table>

Famous People

The following alphabetical list of names includes personalities who are associated with Canada through birth, visit, influence or death and have achieved international importance.

Born in Alliston/Ontario Frederick Grant Banting began to practise in 1920 after studying medicine and specialising in orthopaedics. A year later he carried out research at the University of Toronto with J.J.R. Macleod and with C.H. Best into the secretions of the pancreas. Although his thesis could not be substantiated, his research stimulated more extensive studies which finally led to the discovery of insulin in 1921/22 by a team made up of Macleod, Banting, J.B. Collip and Best.

Sir Frederick Grant Banting
Medical researcher
(1891–1941)

Insulin immediately became effective as a life-saving treatment for diabetes. Banting was acknowledged as its main discoverer, because his idea had given rise to the research, because he was well known for having made early use of insulin, and because he and his friends led a smear campaign against their former colleagues, Macleod and Collip. When he was awarded the Nobel Prize for physiology or medicine he gave half of the prize money to Best. Banting received a life pension from the federal government and was appointed the first Canadian professor of medical research at Toronto university. In 1934 he was knighted. He was killed in an air crash in 1941.

Alexander Graham Bell was born in Edinburgh and arrived in Brantford/Ontario, where he and his father worked as speech therapists for the deaf-mute. Between 1874 and 1876 Bell developed equipment which constituted the first usable telephone. Bell patented his discovery and promoted the commercial use of the telephone in the USA, through which he grew rich. He finally settled in Baddeck/Nova Scotia.

Alexander Graham Bell
Inventor
(1847–1922)

Bell spent the remainder of his life on scientific research and financed other research. He worked on the photo cell, the iron lung, the desalification of seawater and tried to breed a "super race" of sheep. His wife Mabel Gardiner Hubbar (1857–1923) shared his scientific interests. She was a member of the Aerial Experiment Assn., carried out gardening experiments and supported women's right to vote.

The Aerial Experiment Assn. was founded by Bell together with J.A. D. McCurdy, F.W. Baldwin and others. They built some successful, petrol-driven double deckers. The flight of the Silver Dart on February 23rd, 1909 was regarded as the first manned flight in Canada. The company also worked on hydrofoils. The HD-4 set a world record in 1919 with a speed of 114 kmh (71 mph).

Right from being a teenager J. Armand Bombardier attempted to realise his idea of making an all-terrain vehicle, for bog or snow. In 1937 he was successful with his machine which was chain-driven and steered by skis. In 1959 Bombardier's firm brought a Ski-Doo onto the market, a vehicle which created a new type of sport. The size, which was about the same as that of a motorcycle, was new and it was driven by a single large track. Within a short time the vehicle changed the lives of the Inuit and Arctic communities.

J. Armand Bombardier
Inventor
(1908–1964)

Ozias Leduc encouraged the young Paul-Émile Borduas to study at the École des Beaux-Arts in Montréal (1923–27) and helped him with his first visit to Paris (1928–30) in the studio of the Art Sacré, which was led by Maurice Denis.

Paul-Émile Borduas
Painter
(1905–1960)

On returning to Canada he had to give up his dream of becoming a

Famous People

Alexander Graham Bell

Jacques Cartier

Glenn Herbert Gould

church artist like Leduc, as he had to earn his living as an art teacher. In 1937 he became professor at the École du Meuble. During this time he painted very little and destroyed much of his work. His painting was figurative and gradually became more influenced by Renoir, Pascin, James Wilson Morrice and later Cézanne. In 1942 influenced by the Surrealism of André Breton he completed several abstract guaches.

Borduas was increasingly influential with younger painters, especially his students, and he became leader of the Automatist movement. In 1948 he published the manifesto "Refus Global" in which he denounced the oppressive power of established thought in Québec and proclaimed total freedom in art. As a result he had to give up teaching.

From 1953 to 1955 Borduas lived in New York where he was influenced by Action painting. Next he went to Paris. In his painting he concentrated on the contrast between black and white ("L'Étoile noire" of 1957 is considered his masterpiece). Although he was successful in Canada he had difficulty in getting into the art scene in Paris. He dreamed of returning to Canada, but died in 1960.

Examples of his work hang in the National Gallery of Canada, the Musée d'Art Contemporaine and in the Musée des Beaux Arts in Montréal.

John Cabot
Explorer
(1449/50 to 1489/99)

Born Giovanni Caboto (John Cabot) in Genoa, he was the first to prove that his expedition reached North America. Independent of Columbus he seemed to have the idea of reaching Asia by travelling west over the Atlantic.

In 1484 Giovanni Caboto moved to London with his family. In 1496 Henry VII granted him and his sons permission to undertake expeditions of discovery. With a small ship and a crew of 18 men he set sail on May 2nd. In June he landed on the coast of North America, probably either in Newfoundland, South Labrador or Cape Breton Island. He claimed the land in the name of Henry VII and returned home convinced that he had discovered the north-east coast of Asia. The following year he sailed along the east coast of Greenland, which he named Labrador. Later the name was given to a part of the Canadian coast, because it was believed that it belonged to Greenland.

Cabot's journeys formed the basis for England's claim to North America and led to the opening-up of the fishing grounds in the Northwest Atlantic.

Emily Carr
Painter, author
(1871–1945)

Emily Carr, born in the small island town of Victoria to English parents, studied art at the California School of Design in San Francisco after she was orphaned. When she returned home after 2½ years she set up a studio and gave children art lessons. Study leave in England did little for her creativity. A visit to France in 1910/1911 had a stronger impact which was expressed in a post Impressionist style, marking the end of the early English water colour fashion.

In 1908 she began to look for Indian towns to paint the diminishing number of settlements, houses and totem poles.

At 57 she took part in a national exhibition in eastern Canada and met members of the Group of Seven. This was the period of maturity and individual work on which her reputation was later to be founded. From 1932 onwards she gradually received critical acclaim, had national exhibitions and occasionally sold a painting. After 1932 the Indian theme was replaced by subjects from nature and forests, beaches and the sky were freely represented in her paintings. Following a heart attack in 1937 her health began to deteriorate and she devoted more time to writing. In 1941 "Klee Wyck" was published and received the Governor General's Award. She died four years later in her hometown, Victoria.

Jacques Cartier can only be credited with discovering the small area of Québec, which was then called Canada by the Indians. In 1534 he was commissioned by François I to search for the passage to Asia and find gold. He reached Newfoundland and attempting to find a way through the continent discovered the Gulf of St Lawrence. He undertook further expeditions in search of gold and diamonds and came across the St Lawrence River. He was held in high regard when he died in 1557 and was buried in the cathedral of his home town, St Malo.

Jacques Cartier
Explorer
(1491–1557)

The central role played by Samuel de Champlain in discovering the St Lawrence region brought him the nickname "Father of New France".

Samuel de Champlain
Explorer
(c. 1570–1635)

Little is known of his childhood and youth. He was born c. 1570 in Brouage, Normandy, the son of a fisherman. In 1603 he sailed up the St Lawrence River with François Gravé Du Pont. He made the first detailed description of the river since Jacques Cartier's discoveries. A year later Champlain sailed with De Monts to Acadia, where they founded Port-Royal (Annapolis Royal) and Ste-Croix. As a cartographer he was commissioned to find the ideal site for a settlement on the coast. He explored the coast of New England and finally, on De Monts' instruction, founded Québec.

Champlain built up an extensive trade network, forming links with the Montagnais on the St Lawrence, the population around Ottawa and the Huron of the Great Lakes.

Despite the resistance of several trading companies only concerned with the profitable fur trade, Champlain planned to make Québec the centre of a powerful colony. His dream seemed to come true with the founding of the "Compagnie de Cent-Associés" in 1627. But then Québec was occupied by the English from 1629 to 1632. Appointed lieutenant by Cardinal Richelieu, Champlain returned to Québec in 1633, where his plans gradually took shape. He died, however, on December 25th, 1635.

Champlain left various writings about his travels. His works contain the only account of colonisation of the St Lawrence River in the first quarter of the 17th c. He illustrated his descriptions with many maps which record all contemporary knowledge of North America.

The Viking Leif Erikson, son of Erich the Red, was probably the first European to set foot, around the year 1000, on North American soil. His father came to Greenland in 982, where he founded two settlements, which disappeared without explanation in the 14th c.

Leif Erikson
Explorer
(10/11th c.)

He probably landed in the north of Newfoundland "Vinland", where the Norwegian archaeologist Helge Ingstad discovered eight houses with workshops and forges in L'Anse-aux-Meadows between 1960 and 1969.

Two further discoveries, Helluland (land with flat stones) is Baffin Island and Markland (land of forest) is present day Labrador.

Famous People

Sir Sandford
Fleming
Engineer
(1827–1915)

Sandford Fleming was Canada's leading railway inspector in the 19th c. and an outstanding inventor and scientist.

When he arrived in Canada from Scotland in 1845 he continued studying engineering. After gaining professional expertise in railway construction he finally became involved as an engineer in the planning of the line from Québec City to Halifax and Saint John and in 1871 in the planning of the new Canadian railway from Montréal to the Pacific coast. Although his suggested routes for the last project were not adopted, his extensive reports on the various stretches, e.g. Kicking Horse Pass, through which the main route of the Canadian Pacific was built, greatly assisted the construction of the Canadian railways. He resigned from the CPR when the government awarded the project to a private syndicate in 1880.

Fleming turned his interest to other areas. He was an ardent defender of the long distance cable from Canada to Australia, laid in 1902. He was a participant in the International Prime Meridian Conference in Washington in 1884, when standard time was introduced, which still operates today. Fleming also designed the first Canadian stamp, the "3-penny beaver", which came out in 1851.

Simon Fraser
Explorer
fur trader
(1776–1862)

Simon Fraser was born in Mapletown near Bennington in 1776. He was the youngest son of an officer in the government troops, who was taken prisoner by rebels and died in captivity. His mother brought him to Montréal where he was brought up by his uncle.

In 1801 Fraser became a partner in the Athabaska Dept. He was responsible for business beyond the Rockies and founded the earliest settlement in that region, which he named New Caledonia. He established Fort McLeod in 1805, Fort St James and Fraser in 1806 and Fort George (today Prince George) the following year. In 1808 he set off to discover the river which he assumed to be the Columbia. He crossed unknown land fighting his way through dangerous country, today called Fraser River Canyon. On realising that it was not the Columbia he returned deeply disappointed. He wrote a report on his expedition entitled, "The Letters and Journals of Simon Fraser, 1806–08", which are still published today.

Fraser then turned his attention to the fur trade. He was one of the NWC officers, taken prisoner by Lord Selkirk in 1816 and charged with complicity in the Seven Oaks Incident; Fraser was finally acquitted. He died in 1862 in St Andrews.

Glenn Herbert
Gould
Pianist, composer
(1932–1982)

The works of Glenn Herbert Gould, born on 25.9.1932 in Toronto, are of unique importance in the history of music.

He received his musical education at the Royal Conservatorium of Music in Toronto. At the age of 14 he was already a concert soloist with the symphony orchestra there. Solo concerts, performances with many Canadian orchestras and broadcasts on CBC along with his predilection for unusual piano pieces (Bach, 16th c. English piano pieces, modern composers such as Hindesmith and Schönberg) soon made him into one of Canada's leading musicians. His first appearances in Washington and New York in January 1955 and his first recording in the USA that year (Bach's Goldberg variations) brought him international acclaim. Concerts in England, Australia, Germany, Israel and the USSR (where he was one of the first Canadians to go on tour) followed. In 1964 Gould withdrew from the concert stage: he wanted to devote himself to producing records and television programmes.

Gould's talent on the piano was characterised by exceptional linear details and strong movements. His classical interpretations were often provocative and sometimes eccentric in tempo and expression. His repertoire of records contained practically all piano works by Bach and Beethoven, many by Mozart, many from the first half of the 20th c. but few from the 19th century.

Gould wrote articles about all aspects of concert life including such admired pop stars as Barbara Streisand and Petula Clark. He also composed scores for US and Canadian films.

Through his unusual views, his unconventional style and his philosophical observations on music Gould became an institution in the world of pianists.

Anne Hébert's father Maurice, a provincial state official and author, accompanied her in the initial stages of her literary career. Through her mother she was related to the historian François-Xavier Garneau (19th c.). She continued the literary tradition of her family in a spectacular manner.

Hébert grew up in Québec and studied there. From 1950 to 1954 she worked on Radio Canada and wrote plays for NFB. Then she received a scholarship to work in Paris where she lived for a few decades.

In 1942 she published her first collection under the title "Les Songes en équilibre". Her first volume of prose "Le Torrent", which appeared in 1950, shocked the public but became a classic. In 1970 she demonstrated her impressive virtuosity in her major novel "Kamouraska" in which she skilfully combined two plots, set in 19th c. Québec. The novel received the French Prix des Libraires and was filmed by Claude Jutra. She has written many plays, published under the title "Le Temps Sauvage". Hébert's literary career, distinguished by several awards, e.g. the Molson prize, was founded on a life completely devoted to writing. Her literature was a model for other writers.

*Anne Hébert
Author
(b. 1916)*

Little is known about Henry Hudson from the time before his journeys of 1607 to 1611. During the years 1607 and 1608 he twice searched for a route across Norway and Russia to Asia. Commissioned by the Dutch East India Co. he travelled up the Hudson River in 1609. He sailed to Iceland and then into the Hudson Strait. He travelled along the east coast to James Bay which he criss-crossed in a vain attempt to find a passage to the Spice Islands. When he wanted to continue the search in the spring of 1611 his crew mutinied. The leaders of the uprising put Hudson, his son and seven others in a boat on the open sea. Nothing is known about his fate. Hudson did not discover the Hudson Strait – it was Frobisher and Davis – but by taking the dangerous option he left his predecessors far behind and discovered a route into the interior which was of incalculable importance to England.

*Henry Hudson
Explorer
(c. 1550–1611)*

Born in Rouen, France René Robert Cavalier de LaSalle was brought up by Jesuits and practised the priesthood for several years until giving it up in 1667. Then he came to Canada and settled in Montréal. He acquired a piece of land, which he later called Lachine, because of his ambition to reach China by crossing the western oceans.

Fur trading and exploration led LaSalle to Lake Erie and the Ohio River in 1669 and in 1771 to the region south of the Great Lakes. In 1673 he led the construction of Fort Frontenac and eventually became its commander. The following year he was ennobled. In 1678 he began the search for the mouth of the Mississippi; in 1682 he travelled down the river from Illinois to the Gulf of Mexico and called the land Louisiana. Two years later he led an expedition by boat to found a colony in Louisiana. As the mouth of the Mississippi was not discovered the colonists went ashore on the coast of present day Texas. After vain attempts to find the delta from the sea, led his group overland to the river. However, some settlers mutinied and murdered him.

*René Robert
Cavalier Sieur
de LaSalle
Explorer
(1643–1687)*

Sir Wilfrid Laurier was born in Laurentides north of Montréal. After studying he became a lawyer. His political career began in 1874: Laurier became a Member of the Canadian parliament; in 1887 he took over the leadership of the Liberal Party. From 1896 to 1911 he was prime minister, the first French-Canadian to hold this office.

Laurier devoted his entire life to the service of Canadian unity. Under

*Sir Wilfrid Laurier
Politician
(1841–1919)*

Famous People

his leadership Canada prospered. It was he, above all, who oversaw mass immigration and the settlement of the Canadian west.

Sir John Alexander Macdonald
Lawyer, politician, businessman
(1815–1891)

John Alexander Macdonald was brought by his parents to Kingston/Upper Canada when he was five. At 15 he was articled to a prominent lawyer and opened his own legal practice at 19. He was a practising lawyer all his life, specialising in economic law. From the 1840s he was engaged in various business activities. He dealt in real estate, bought land in many parts of the province and was director of some companies.

He played an increasingly active role in conservative politics and in 1844 was elected to the legislative body of the province of Canada. Together with Étienne-Paschal Taché he became prime minister of the province in 1856. He was involved in the plan for a federal system, in which the central government had clear control over the provincial governments. Through his constitutional expertise, his abilities and his knowledge he won the recognition of the British colonial government. He was knighted and elected the first Canadian prime minister in 1867.

During his first period in office from 1867 to 1873 Manitoba, the Northwest Territories (now Saskatchewan and Alberta), British Columbia and Prince Edward Island joined the first four provinces. His government had to resign under suspicion of corruption in connection with planning the Canadian Pacific Railway and suffered defeat in the 1874 election.

Four years later he became prime minister again and remained in office until the end of his life. In 1879 he introduced his National policy, whereby high import taxes were applied to foreign goods to protect the domestic economy. The major national project of his second period of office was the completion of the transcontinental Canadian Pacific Railway, an extremely difficult and expensive undertaking, which required enormous public subsidies. The first steps towards greater autonomy in international affairs were taken. Against his intentions the central government lost power in the federal system.

Alexander Mackenzie
Explorer
(1755? to 1820)

The second longest river in North America and an enormous area of northern Canada (District of Mackenzie) are named after the explorer Alexander Mackenzie.

Mackenzie is thought to have been born in Inverness, Scotland; at the age of 10 he came with his father to New York. He quickly took over control of the Montréal Company – later North West Company – which he joined in 1779. The company's aim was to explore the north-west of Canada, and Mackenzie was obsessed with the idea of finding a way from eastern Canada to the Pacific. Under his command an expedition set out on June 30th 1798, which after 100 days and 3000 kilometres terminated not at the Pacific but at the Arctic Ocean. Mackenzie did not give up and set off again in July 1792 with a team to find the Northwest Passage. This time he was successful: on July 22nd 1793 Mackenzie and his team reached the coast of the Pacific Ocean north of Vancouver Island. In so doing Mackenzie succeeeded in making the first known crossing of the North American continent; he made a huge contribution to the geographical and cartographical opening up of the country. His diaries (Voyages from Montréal, on the River St Lawrence, through the continent of North America), first published in London in 1802, are filled with impressions and extraordinarily detailed observations.

William Lyon Mackenzie
Journalist, politician
(1795–1861)

William Lyon Mackenzie, journalist, first mayor of Toronto and leader of the 1837 rebellion, was a central figure in political life before the confederation.

He was born in Dundee, Scotland on March 12th 1795. He came to Upper Canada in 1820 and after a few years in Dundas moved to Queenston. In May 1820 he published the first edition of "Colonial Advocate", which became a leading voice in the new reform movement. In 1824 Mackenzie went to York (Toronto). In 1828 he was elected to the assembly of York district.

Mackenzie's severe attacks on the local oligarchy resulted in libel cases against him, threats and physical injury and led to his repeated expulsion from the assembly; yet his rural voters remained loyal to him. In 1834, when the Reform party won the majority in the newly constituted town council of Toronto, Mackenzie was elected the first mayor. However, he lost the 1836 election. In 1837 he led an armed revolt. After its defeat he fled to the USA, where he continued to campaign to "Free Upper Canada" until he was imprisoned for violating the neutrality laws. Mackenzie spent the next ten years in exile in the USA. Finally he found a position as correspondent for the "New York Daily Tribune".

Louis-Joseph de Montcalm, born in Candiac, France, who joined the army at the age of nine, was appointed commander of the French troops in North America. He conquered Fort William Henry in 1757 and resisted a British attack on Fort Carillon in 1758.

Marquis Louis Joseph de Montcalm Commander (1712–1759)

In 1759, owing to a miscalculation by the French, Wolfe landed with 4500 soldiers on the Plains of Abraham, less than 2 km (1½ mil.) from Québec. Montcalm quickly stationed his troops for the defensive battle. The French were beaten and Montcalm fatally wounded.

Historians are of the opinion that Montcalm achieved some worthy victories but also suffered the worst defeat in Canadian military history.

Louis Riel, born in the Red River Settlement, first studied for the priesthood then law.

Louis Riel Leader of the Métis, founder of Manitoba (1844–1885)

He played a crucial role in the North West rebellion of 1869/1870. He supported the cause of the Métis even when it came to armed struggles. At the finish he fled to the USA but soon returned. He was successful in the 1874 election but was sentenced to two years imprisonment and the loss of his political rights for his part in the rebellion. In 1875 he was granted an amnesty on condition that he stayed in exile for five years.

Shortly afterwards he suffered a nervous breakdown and was taken to a psychiatric clinic. By nature introspective and strictly religious he was obsessed by the thought of introducing a new Catholicism to Canada. On his release from the clinic he went to the Upper Missouri region of Montana where he traded. He joined the Republican party, became an American citizen and married a Métis. In 1883 he became a teacher in the St Peter mission on the Sun river. As he was asked by a group of Canadian Métis to support their struggle for rights in Saskatchewan he moved to Batoche, the centre of the Métis. This conflict also ended in armed resistance in 1885 and ended with defeat for the Métis. A formal charge of treason was then made against him and he was sentenced to death.

Politically and philosophically the execution of Riel had a long-lasting effect on Canadian history. In the west many Métis were disillusioned, whereas in Central Canada French Canadian nationalism was strengthened. Even after a century Riel is still the topic of heated debate, especially in Québec and Manitoba. His execution is a controversial subject and there are still those who demand retrospective compensation.

Gabrielle Roy, winner of the Governor General's Award (1947, 1957, 1978) and many other literary commendations in Canada and abroad (Lorne Pierce Medal 1947; Prix Duvernay 1956; Prix David 1971), is one of Canada's most important post-war female writers.

Gabrielle Roy Author (1909–1963)

She was the youngest of eight children in a francophone family in St Boniface and lived until 1937 in Manitoba. She was strongly influenced by the Prairie landscape and the cosmopolitan thinking of the immigrants who had settled in western Canada in the early 20th c.

When Roy had finished her studies she taught in school for twelve years. In 1937 she went to Europe. During the two years she was in France and England she began to write. The imminent war forced her to return to Canada. She became a freelance journalist in Montréal.

Her novel "Bonheur d'occasion" (The Tin Flute), published in 1945, in which the lives of the working class in the early period of the war are described, won the Prix Fémina in Paris and the Literary Guild of America Award in New York. It was translated into more than 15 languages and established her literary fame. Following another visit to France she settled in Québec. She wrote about the loneliness of modern life ("Alexandre Chenevert", 1954), the obsessive creativity of the artist ("La Montagne Secrète", 1961), the conflict between traditional and modern values ("La rivière sans repos", 1970), the poetry of nature ("Cet été qui chantait", 1972), immigration ("Un Jardin au bout du monde", 1975) and specially about her own youth ("Rue Deschambault", 1955; "La Route d'Altamont", 1966; "Ces enfants de ma vie", 1977). Roy's works, written in a plain and simple style, have a varied public, both in Canada, where her books are translated into English, and abroad. Her central theme concerns people in pain and loneliness which are eased by the love implicit in creation, and the hope for a world in which all people live together in harmony.

Sir George Simpson
Managing director of the Hudson's Bay Company
(c. 1787–1860)

George Simpson from Lochbroom, Scotland was sent by the Hudson's Bay Company of London in 1820 to take over the post of the managing director, who had been captured by the North West Company. On the amalgamation of the two companies in 1821 he first was in control of the large Northern Department and five years later over the whole trading territory in British North America. He retained this position until his death. Simpson wrote extensive reports, e.g. "Narrative of a Journey Round the World, During the Years 1841 and 1842". He was knighted at this time for his contribution to Arctic exploration.

Simpson knew the fur trade like nobody else. He was a capable administrator and indefatigable traveller who, at the same time, did not lose sight of his own interests.

George Vancouver
Explorer
(1757–1798)

Born in King's Lynn, England on June 22nd 1757, George Vancouver accompanied James Cook to the South Seas (1772–75) and to the Northwest coast (1776–80).

He had two missions: he was to win back the British possession Nootka Sound, conquered by the Spanish, and explore the Californian coast as far as Cook Inlet. His negotiations with the Spanish were unsuccessful. He spent three summers exploring the coast.

In 1795 he returned to England and three years later published "A Voyage of Discovery to the North Pacific Ocean and Round the World". He claimed to have removed all doubt about the existence of a northwest passage from the Atlantic to the Pacific.

James Wolfe
Commander
(1727/1728 to 1759)

James Wolfe rose to fame through his victory over Montcalm in 1759, which marked the start of British rule over Canada.

He came to North America in 1758 and took part as leading officer in the campaign by Jeffery Amherst against Louisbourg, in which he played a major role. He was therefore named commander of the campaign against Québec, which was planned for the following year. Here he had little success. His stormed attack on Montmorency was a big mistake, and neither the bombardment of Québec nor the destruction of neighbouring settlements had any effect. On the suggestion of his officers he planned to land above the town to cut off supply lines and to bring about a battle. So after a nocturnal trip on the St Lawrence, he led his army on to the Plains of Abraham, where Montcalm's troops were attacked and beaten by the British. Wolfe was fatally wounded.

Culture

Art History

There are three main multicultural influences on Canadian art history. Firstly, the Inuit, the original inhabitants of the north, who still today play a major part in artistic creativity (especially sculpture and painting). In second place are the Indians, but whose influence is constantly diminishing. Thirdly are the immigrants (Europeans in particular, but also Asians of different backgrounds) who have been streaming into the country since the 17th c.

Note

Although it is not possible to define the various Inuit cultures exactly, five periods can be determined:

Inuit

The pre-Dorset culture began with the arrival of people who had crossed the Bering Strait from Siberia 4000 years ago. Only a few works of art have been found from this period, but they are outstanding. They mostly consist of harpoon tips and spears from carefully selected stones, which were not only functional but were also of considerable aesthetic value and were also attributed magical properties. The pre-Dorset culture lasted over 1000 years.

Pre-Dorset

Dorset culture began to develop between 600 and 500 BC and can be described as the first indigenous, Canadian-Arctic culture. It spread from Coronation Gulf to the southern tip of Newfoundland and to the west coast of Greenland. The highly developed Dorset culture seems to have had extensive magical and religious aims. For example, there were harpoon tips in the shape of impaled bears and falcons. The pattern on the carved animals must have had some special significance.

Dorset

Other types of art objects were discovered: faces carved from antlers or wood, wooden masks, human figures, animal paintings and objects of various birds and mammals. While their purpose is for the main part unknown they share certain features: most are carved in ivory; they are very small (about 1 to 10 centimetres (½ to 4 in.)), and all are very expressively worked.

The Thule culture from north Alaska began to penetrate the Canadian Arctic after 1000 AD and reached east Greenland about 1200.

Thule culture

It is the most united Inuit culture and was spread across the Arctic to the eastern tip of Siberia.

The most common evidence of Thule culture in Canada are combs, needle cases, "swimming figurines" (birds, spirits and people) which were probably intended as amulets or had similar magical and religious properties, together with assorted female statues and utensils. Unlike the Dorset culture, the objects of art of the Thule culture are female in nearly every detail. The female figurines and statuettes are small, finely worked and often beautifully decorated, yet interestingly have no carved face.

The Historic period began in the 16th c. as more Europeans advanced into the Arctic. At the beginning of the 19th c. quality dolls, toys and carved animals were produced for barter. Around 1920 the works of art made primarily from ivory or bone had lost all their magical and religious significance. Although the Inuit maintained a traditional lifestyle before the Second World War, their artistic forms – but not their technique – adapted to suit the taste of the potential buyers.

Historic period

Art History

This phase coincided with the gradual opening up of the north after the Second World War and especially with the interest of Europe and North America in the art of prehistoric and early societies. Contemporary Inuit art can be traced back to the initiatives of the painter and writer James Houston, who was supported by the Canadian government. It was not least because of his decisive involvement that Inuit craftwork became remarkably successful within a short space of time.

In the north of Québec province, later also on Baffin Island, the Inuit have become familiar with different printing techniques (lithography, copper engraving, etching) and have continued carving in soapstone, ivory and antler bone and prepared decorative pelts (wall hangings, coats made of different furs and with borders), appliqué and embroidery in silk and cotton.

Inuit art is mainly of a narrative or illustrative nature. Traditional lifestyles, survival techniques, animals of the north (and their souls) and myths are reflected in their art. Exceptional artists are: Aqguhadluq, Aqjangajuk Shaa (b. 1937), Qaqaq Ashoona (b. 1933), Pauta Saila and Parr (1893–1969).

Today the works of the Inuit are regarded as an important contribution by Canada to the development of modern art, although the motifs are, for the main part, taken from traditional Arctic life.

The contemporary phase developed and changed very quickly. Collectors and museums pay exceptionally high prices for older objects and prints, and the production of new art is increasing to a great extent but leading to a fall in quality.

The most significant collection of contemporary Inuit art is housed in the Winnipeg Art Gallery.

The history of Indian art began about 25,000 years ago with the immigration of the original North American population across the Bering Strait into modern day Canada. Whereas the Indians' first contact with the French occurred in the early 16th c. in the Lake provinces and in the St Lawrence Valley, the Indians of the west coast did not see any Europeans until the late 18th c. The earliest evidence are rock drawings, which are still visible on some lakesides (especially in southern Ontario).

Prehistoric art varies in genre, style, function, imagery and meaning, not only from region to region, but has changed from period to period. These changes were apparent throughout Canada from c. 1000 BC onwards as a consequence of different factors: the introduction of pottery, the beginning of land cutivation and settling down.

There were some outstanding periods of prehistoric art in Canada. The Marpole culture (c. 500 BC to 500 AD), which was concentrated around the Fraser delta and the nearby islands in southern British Columbia, produced a wide variety of stone and bone carving (ceremonial containers, portraits and utensils).

The early Iroquois culture (c. 900–1600 AD) in southern Ontario is characterised by pottery of technical quality and with symbolic geometric patterns. The Iroquois art of the upper St Lawrence Valley is known for its decorated clay and stone pipes which display a fascinating wealth of form and iconographic variety. These miniature masterpieces had a sacred function: the ritual smoking of tobacco as part of the Indian system of cultural beliefs.

The art of the eastern sub-Arctic is the most archaic in Canada; a large part of prehistoric and early rock painting was found in this region. Most of the Algonquin-speaking tribes – the Ojibwa, Cree, Algonquin, Ottawa, Montagnais, the Naskapi of Ontario and Québec together with the Mic-Mac and Maliset of the southern lake provinces – continued to lead a nomadic life, based on hunting and gathering food.

The Mic-Mac were famous for their embroidery with elk hair and for engraving with porcupine quills on birch bark as well as basket-making and leather and textile clothing. Glass pearls, brought by the European

Totem poles of the Indians of the north-west coast in Vancouver and Kisplox, B.C.

traders, replaced the elk hair and feathers, which were difficult to work, but changed the patterns.

The Naskapi made exquisite coats from caribou leather (carved or painted linear and geometric patterns).

The works of art of the Ojibwa women were similar to those in the sub-Arctic region: decorations of feathers and beads on clothes and basket-weaving with geometric and floral patterns. The men were responsible for ceremonial objects.

The work of the Cree was noted for its exquisite feather and elk hair embroidery, regarded for its technical perfection and colour harmony. As these nomadic hunters carried their possessions with them, articles of clothing, especially their decorated and embroidered coats, mocassins and hunting gloves, were an expression of their own aesthetic taste.

Among some tribes of the western sub-Arctic decoration of personal possessions was the most important art form. These tribes decorated caribou and elk leather using porcupine quills, elk hair embroidery, beads and stitching (also geometric and floral patterns).

As the Iroquois speaking people of the south Great Lakes and the upper St Lawrence Valley (Hurons, Neutals, Petuns and Iroquois among others) were practically settled farmers, living in villages, this was reflected in their artistic forms of expression. Whereas there was considerable homogenity on the whole with the bead and feather work in the sub-Arctic and at the Great Lakes, Huron art became distinctive in the later historic periods. Their "personal art" displayed a preference for elk hair embroidery with flower motifs on black coloured leather of exceptional beauty. The most remarkable art form of the Iroquois consisted of "false masks" , wooden masks with metal eyes used for healing ceremonies. Other objects with "political" function were the wampum cords and belts made of purple and white shells. These wampums with their symbolic motifs denoted treaties and important events.

Art History

The culture of the Prairie Indians was a synthesis of native and white culture. Their most important art form was painted leather and the most important architectural form the "tepee" tent. Buckskin shoes (moccasins), jackets, clothes, leggings and shirts were decorated with feathers and beads. Painted cooking pots, containers from uncured leather were produced throughout his region.

The plateau region in central British Columbia is often overlooked in descriptions of Indian art, but in many ways it is unique. The Salish left behind a mass of prehistoric pictographs. The Lillooet, Thompson, Okanagan, and Shuswap of the historical period were renowned for their finely worked waterproof baskets (weaving technique, geometric patterns).

The Indian art of the prehistoric period and the colonial period was to a certain extent "traditional". Although it was widely influenced by European materials, techniques and patterns in the historic periods, it was still much characterised by Indian cultures.

Contemporary art

As with the Inuit after the Second World War contemporary Indian art developed which employed modern techniques, but also fell back on traditional subjects from mythology, tribal history and hunting and everyday customs.

Contemporary Indian art has two main centres, the west coast and the forest lands of eastern Canada. The latter became famous through the success of Ojibwa Norval Morisseau (b. 1932). Most forestland artists are influenced by Morisseau. They are known as the "legend painters" as they represent stories and mythology in their works (Carl Ray, Daphne Odjig, Blake Debassige).

The international artists regard themselves as being independent of every "school". However, their pictures clearly illustrate in their form and content the connection with their Indian origins. Outstanding artists from this group are: Alex Janvier, Arthur Schilling (famous Ojibwa portraits) and Sarain Stump (symbolic Surrealist works). The images of life in the reservations by Allen Sapp are reminiscent of 19th c. realism and are typical of the conservative trend among Indian artists.

Paintings, prints and sculptures by Canadian Indians have meanwhile become expensive collectors' items.

Many historical artefacts of the Cree, Ojibwa, Shoshone, Blackfoot, Chipewayan, Kwakiuti, etc. are exhibited in Ottawa, Toronto and Calgary. Contemporary works are on display in the National Gallery in Ottawa and Calgary.

Immigrant art

Early Canadian art followed European traditions. The first representations of natives on maps were shaped more by imported prejudice than knowledge of the discoverers. Illustrations in the first books about Canada were more accurate. Some sketches in the works of Samuel Champlain convey meaningful insights into the life of the Hurons.

17–18th century

French mercantile activity impeded the development of painting in Canada. With the exception of votive pictures and some portraits of nuns and officers, paintings were imported during French rule.

The arrival of the British in North America had a direct effect on the development of painting. English officers demonstrated their enthusiasm for Canada in their topographical drawings and ornamental landscapes. Thomas Davies was one of the earliest and most important of these English water-colour painters.

The influence of new waves of immigrants was felt on Canadian art. The English preferred Georgian style for a long time, which even later still symbolised the association with the English crown. The Loyalists brought works of art and ideas from the USA, e.g. silver, engravings and paintings.

19th century

Around 1900 increasing prosperity promoted education of the middle classes and the development of some garrison communities. Portraits of businessmen and their families, of soldiers, government officials and clerics were in demand. Robert Field was a brilliant artist, who was familiar with contemporary styles and techniques.

The turn of the century marked the beginning of the so-called Golden Age of Québec painting. The artists there went to Europe to study, and European artists came to Canada. Antoine Plamondon and Théophile Hamel (1817–70) belonged to the first group, William Berczy (1744–1813) and Cornelius Krieghoff (1815–72) to the second. Educated in Düsseldorf Krieghoff painted romantic scenes from everyday life and landscapes. Joseph Légaré also created landscapes and portrayed dramatic events from the history of Québec.

Stylistically the European influence in Canada continued to be dominant, but the spectrum of subjects in painting widened. Peter Rindisbacher (1806–34) depicted his experiences as an immigrant in small pictures. Paul Kane (1810–71) can be described as an artist/adventurer: on a journey through Canada in 1846 he recorded the Indians and countryside in 240 sketches and 100 pictures.

Among the portrait painters was G.T. Berthon (1806–92), landscape artists included Robert R. Whale and discoverer/painter William Hind (1833–89). They were all predecessors to the more notable Lucius O'Brien (1832–99), John A. Fraser (1838–98) and Allan Edson (1846–88), who favoured romantic landscapes.

With the confederation in 1867 art was to express the new feeling of unity. Robert Harris (1849–1919) was commissioned to paint his famous group portrait "The Fathers of Confederation" (1882). In 1880 the National Gallery of Canada was founded by the Marquis de Lorne.

Around the turn of the century painting was represented by such important artists as James Wilson Morrice (1865–1924), the father of Canadian modernism; Ozias Leduc (1864–1955), who created ambitious church decorations and exquisite still lifes and landscapes around St Hilaire; Homer Watson (1855–1936), who conveyed an intimate observation of landscape; as well as George Reid (1860–1947) and Paul Peel (1860–92), who were closer to academic tradition. The early Twenties were a great time for Canadian painting. The "Group of Seven", who saw it as their task to give Canada a real national style of painting, regarded the Canadian countryside as source of their inspiration. They used strong colours to represent this decoratively. Tom Thomson (1877–1917), despite his short career, left behind a surprising number of pictures and sketches in oil.

Emily Carr (1871–1945), influenced by the Fauvists, was the first female artist to receive high acclaim in Canadian art.

John Lyman (1866–1967) tried to set up an artistic movement from the École de Paris in the early Thirties. In 1939 he founded the Contemporary Arts Society and organised a modern offensive in Canadian painting.

During the Second World War painting in Canada advanced in an exemplary way. Shortly after his return from Paris Alfred Pellan (b. 1906) made the effects of Cubism (especially of Pablo Picasso) felt. Paul-Émile Borduas (1905–60) collected a group of young painters around him, among them, Jean-Paul Riopelle (b. 1923) and Fernand Leduc (b. 1916), and formed the so-called Automatists. The manifesto "Refus Global", which appeared in 1948 and had considerable ideological influence on Québec, marked moderate thinking, free from religious and other conformism. As a reaction to the Automatists the sculptors Guido Molinari (b. 1933) and Claude Tousignant (b. 1932) freed painting from its surrealist constraints and focused on formal styles.

The painters in Toronto followed similar aims. The Painters Eleven, of whom the most famous were Harold Town (b. 1924) and Jack Bush (1909–77) changed from abstract Expressionism, as practised in New York, to Formalism.

The general problem of Canadian painting was to maintain its orig-

20th century

inality faced with the strong American influences. Michael Snow (b. 1929) with his outstanding film contributions and the "London, Ont. Group" with Greg Curnoe and Jack Chambers (1931–78) partly succeeded in standing apart from American art.

Contemporary art in Canada was and is, as is elsewhere, characterised by the question of what constitutes art. This questioning was accompanied by experimentation and innovation. The resulting works varied from the entirely personal to public disagreement with social and political problems. Contemporary art analyses the relationship between means and ends, distinguishes art from reality and defines art in its aesthetic, social and economic contexts. In Canada the multitude of contemporary trends was a consequence of the separation of art centres from each other and their different developments.

Fusion des Arts in Montréal (founded. 1964) and Intermedia in Vancouver (founded 1967) originated in this period. They were loose associations of artists who worked in a variety of media (film, music, dance, poetry) as well as in the traditional areas of painting and sculpture. The resulting happenings and performances, which combined touch and sound, watching and movement, were performed in art galleries and elsewhere. They were carried by the optimism surrounding the social gain brought about by art, as they now spoke a common language. Iain (b. 1936) and Ingrid Baxter demonstrated their own multimedia and interdisciplinary principles.

Concept-art represented the view that if traditional forms of painting and sculpture had become meaningless, then the aim was to bring out the essential "art content", which exists independent of all form. More important than the works were the ideas of concept-art. Michael Snow was representative of this direction in art. He experimented with the possibilities of the camera. His work, which won international recognition, inspired many other artists.

Whereas concept-art was concentrated in eastern Canada, body art was the applied form which had the farthest-reaching effects. According to this genre the artist as a person was regarded simultaneously as the source of all ideas and interpreted as the final means of their realisation. In environmental art the perception of the person is expanded to the perception of the environment. The reality "outside" is awarded more weight than its reproduction in painting or other traditional medium. Since the late 1960s this long-lasting artistic direction has been practised (Irene Whittome, Bill Vazan, Rita McKeough).

Collage is celebrating its rediscovery. There should be no more discrimination between objects of art. Everything should play a part in the way we view the world. This idea is also part of structuralism and represented in the works of Michael Morris, Vincent Trasov, Glenn Lewis.

In the late 1970s metaphor re-appeared in art. An intellectial analysis of how modern art can develop and what meaning it can have is featured in the work of Jeff Wall and Ian Wallace.

Performance art was one of the most significant combined art forms. Bruce Barber critically examined the socio-political content of the mass media. The performances were a good medium for conveying feminist ideas (Elizabeth Chitty, Marcella Bienvenue).

Many native artists from all parts of the country were searching for forms, which combined the elements of traditional art and mythology with their own responses to the present. A large number of artists wanted to use all means of finding an uncompromising answer to the "disastrous" world, including traditional painting. Two of these artists are Jamelie Hassam and Ron Benner.

Carol Condé and Karl Beveridge tried, through their photography, to answer the question how, in his compromised position restricted by his privilege, the artist can work. Brian Dyson and Paul Woodrow believed

Evening on the coast of Newfoundland ▶

that direct social activities were the only effective way for artists to realise their ideas.

The earliest Canadian sculpture was sacral art found in the churches and chapels of New France. In the late 17th c. sculptors were commissioned to decorate the churches with carved and gilded altars in wood. As the sculptures, unlike the church paintings, could not be transported by ship very easily, they were produced where they were wanted. The most important artists were the Baillaigrés in Québec and Louis Quévillon (1749–1823) in Montréal. These sculptors followed, with a time delay, the predominant styles of Europe: Louis XV, Rococo, Neo-Classicism.

Following the Naploeonic Wars England expanded its fleet in Canada. Wood carving (figureheads, ship decorations) flourished in Québec and in the Atlantic provinces.

Around the turn of the century sculpture, which until then had followed traditional styles, began to change. New materials were discovered, wood was replaced by bronze and plaster. There was a demand for historic monuments in city centres. After the First World War many towns erected war monuments. The façades of new buildings were decorated. The prime example of this is the façade of the parliamentary building in Québec by Louis-Phillipe Hébert (1850 to 1917). New subjects were absorbed such as Indian and characters from folklore and Canadian history. As in the past styles emerged which copied European trends: Academism, Art Nouveau, Symbolism (Alfred Laliberté; 1878 to 1953) and later Art Deco.

In the 1960s sculptors, like painters, attempted to emphasise their own originality as a reaction to the strong American influences. Examples include: Armand Vaillancourt (b. 1932), Robert Roussil (b. 1925) and Robert Murray (b. 1936).

Michael Snow and numerous other experimented with modern materials. Companies, banks and government departments promoted sculpture in their new buildings.

Suggested Routes

TransCanada Highway

It is possible to drive from east to west (or vice versa) on the 7500 km (4660 mi.) TransCanada Highway that runs from St John's, the capital of Newfoundland, on the Atlantic coast in the extreme east through the Atlantic provinces of Newfoundland, Nova Scotia and New Brunswick, past Québec city to Montréal. It continues via Ottawa, North Bay, Thunder Bay (all three in Ontario province), Winnipeg (Manitoba), Regina (Saskatchewan), Calgary (Alberta) and finally through the Rocky Mountains to Vancouver in the far west on the Pacific coast.

Between five and six weeks should be allowed for the trip from coast to coast. This leaves time to take in the wonderful scenery with all its natural beauty as well as the interesting towns and places of historical significance.

From the Atlantic to the Pacific

The TransCanada Highway begins in the far west of Newfoundland on the Avalon peninsula at the provincial capital St John's. It then follows a westerly, then northern direction to Clarenville where a detour can be made along the south-west pointing peninsula to Burin or Bonavista on the north-eastern cape.

St John's (Newfoundland)– Clarenville (160 km (99 mi.))

From Clarenville it heads northwards through the 400 sq. km (154 sq. mi.) Terra Nova National Park to Gander, famous in the past for its international airport where north Atlantic air traffic refuelled. The route turns off to the west to Grand Falls.

Clarenville– Grand Falls (270 km (168 mi.))

After Grand Falls it continues north again past Notre Dame Bay. Near Springdale turn off in a south-west direction towards Deer Lake. A detour north-west to Gros Morne National Park in the Long Range Mountains is recommended.

Grand Falls– Deer Lake (225 km (140 mi.))

From Deer Lake proceed south-west to St George's and further along St George's Bay, which is part of the Gulf of St Lawrence. The southern slopes of the Long Range Mountains sink down at the channel port of Port-aux-Basques into the Cabot Strait.

Deer Lake– Port-aux-Basques (272 km (169 mi.))

The 170 km (105 mi.)-long ferry journey (5 to 6 hours duration) from the Newfoundland channel port of Port-aux-Basques across the Cabot Strait to North Sydney in Nova Scotia is best undertaken overnight.

Port-aux-Basques –North Sydney (ferry journey)

The initial stage on the Canadian mainland leads first from the ferry port of North Sydney on the north-east tip of Nova Scotia to Sydney. A short detour south-east to the fortifications at Louisbourg is suggested.

North Sydney– Truro (323 km (201 mi.))

From Sydney the TransCanada Highway continues south-west past Antigonish to New Glasgow. From here it is possible to take a boat excursion to the northern off-shore Prince Edward Island. It is not far from New Glasgow to Truro.

A branch road leads from Truro to Halifax, the capital of Nova Scotia, situated in the south.

TransCanada Highway

Truro–Moncton (177 km (110 mi.))	From Truro head north-west to Amherst on the border of Nova Scotia and New Brunswick. It is only ¾ hour to Moncton in the historic region of Acadia.
Moncton– Fredericton (200 km (124 mi.))	From Moncton continue south-west to Sussex (possible detour to New Brunswick port of St John) and then north-west past Grand Lake to Fredericton, the capital of New Brunswick. An alternative to this direct route is a scenic drive along the Bay of Fundy with the Fundy National Park to Sussex. From Sussex drive via St John and then on road 7 north to Fredericton.
Fredericton Grand Falls (210 km (130 mi.))	From Fredericton the route proceeds along the valley of the St John river, past several major hydro energy complexes and along the border with the US state of Maine. Charming places en route are Woodstock and Hartland (with the longest wooden bridge in the world). The road to Grand Falls crosses "Potato country" (immense potato-growing region). The gorge carved out by the St John river and the reservoir at Grand Falls should not be missed.
Grand Falls– Rivière-du-Loup (122 km (76 mi.))	From Grand Falls head north to Edmundston, where many French-speaking Acadians live today. Just before reaching Edmundston it is worth a visit to Restigouche in a north-east direction, and the Baie des Chaleurs with the port of Campbellton. Not far north of Edmundston the road crosses the border between the provinces of New Brunswick and Québec. A few kilometres further lies Cabano with Fort Ingall. Continue through the foothills of the American Appalachians, countryside similar to the Black Forest, and down to the St Lawrence river (Bas-St-Laurent) to Rivière-du-Loup.
Rivière-du-Loup– Lévis/Québec (195 km (121 mi.))	From Rivière-du-Loup drive along the south bank of the St Lawrence upstream through fertile farmland and past friendly fishing villages to Lévis, the heavily industrialised suburb of the provincial capital Québec, on the other bank of the St Lawrence river. A visit to Québec and the region demands at least one or more days.
Lévis/Québec– Montréal (265 km (165 mi.))	From Lévis/Québec continue in a south-westerly direction to Drummondville, the centre of Estrie (=long-established settlement east of Montréal). From here past St Hyacinthe to Montréal, the second largest French-speaking city in the world. A visit to this east Canadian metropolis also requires one or more days.
Montréal–Ottawa (200 km (124 mi.))	From Montréal follow the Ottawa river upstream to the Canadian capital city, Ottawa, situated on the border between the provinces of Québec and Ontario. There is a lot to see here so sufficient time should be allowed. A visit to Ottawa's neighbouring town, Hull, and to Gatineau, the countryside extending northwards is to be recommended.
Ottawa– North Bay (368 km (229 mi.))	The TransCanada Highway follows the Ottawa river from Ottawa and borders on the north side of the Algonquin National Park, finally reaching the prettily situated settlement of North Bay (Ontario) on Lake Nipissing.
North Bay– Kapuskasing (490 km (305 mi.))	From North Bay the route leads into the north of Ontario province, past the mining town of Cobalt and the romantic Esker Lakes to Iroquois Falls and beyond to Cochrane, Ontario. Here the road turns in a north-west direction passing Greenwater Park to Smoky Falls. Destination of this stage is Kapuskasing, Ontario.
Kapuskasing– North Bay (620 km (385 mi.))	Leaving Kapuskasing the road continues through seemingly endless forests west to Lake Nipigon, where there is a beautiful provincial park. It now runs south-west to Nipigon, to the bank of the Upper Lake. This stage ends in Thunder Bay.

National road 17 leads from Thunder Bay through a thinly populated area and through massive forests past Ignace and Dryden to Kenora.

Thunder Bay–Kenora
(510 km (317 mi.))

A 570 km (354 mi.)-long but attractive alternative route runs west past Kabakeka Falls to Atikokan on the northern edge of Quetico Park protected area. It continues west along the small river Seine to the Canadian-US border at Fort Frances. Beyond Fort Frances the national road 17 turns north to Lake of the Woods with the settlement Sioux Narrows. Kenora is a little way ahead.

To the west of Kenora it crosses the border between Ontario and Manitoba, continuing along the southern edge of the Whiteshell Nature Park towards Winnipeg, where a longer stay is suggested. South of Winnipeg, in an area populated by Mennonites, are several German place names (e.g. Steinbach, Winkler, Altona).

Kenora–Winnipeg
(210 km (130 mi.))

The TransCanada Highway continues west from Winnipeg. Near Brandon it is possible to make an excursion to the extremely interesting Riding Mountain National Park, 80 km (50 mi.) north. This stage, however, finishes at Virden.

Winnipeg–Virden
(286 km (177 mi.))

From Virden the route proceeds north-west reaching the border between Manitoba and Saskatchewan after about an hour. It then passes Moosomin, Whitewood, Grenfell and Indian Head before coming to Regina, the capital of Manitoba province, which is worth visiting.

Virden–Regina
(300 km (186 mi.))

The well constructed TransCanada Highway continues west, first to Moose Jaw. At last it becomes obvious that this is the Canadian Prairies. There is a possible detour from Swift Current to the snaking South Saskatchewan river further north and Lake Diefenbaker. Recreational and sports facilities are available here.

Regina–Swift Current
(246 km (152 mi.))

The skyline of Calgary

TransCanada Highway

Swift Current–
Medicine Hat
(223 km (138 mi.))

From Swift Current the Highway heads west-south-west for the border between the provinces of Saskatchewan and Alberta. The Cypress Hills National Park, which is well worth a visit, extends south over the border. Medicine Hat is the destination for this stretch.

Medicine Hat–
Calgary
(295 km (183 mi.))

Travelling north-west from Medicine Hat the landscape becomes rather uninviting. North-east of Brooks a detour leads to the Dinosaur Provincial Park.

North-west of Brooks is Bow river and finally Calgary, the world-famous city of southern Alberta.

Calgary–Banff
(130 km (81 mi))

West of Calgary begins the splendid upland section of the TransCanada Highway. An hour's drive from Calgary is Canmore, famous for the Olympics and winter sports. Beyond Canmore the route enters the Banff National Park. Banff is a sport and outdoor recreation centre.

Banff–Kamloops
(500 km (310 mi.))

The highway winds on from Banff, past the romantic Lake Louise and over Kicking Horse Pass to Yoho National Park and beyond into the wild Kootenay Valley, where the world-famous winter sports resort Golden is situated.

From Golden it climbs steeply uphill and over the chain of the Purcell Mountains, crosses the Glacier National Park and borders on Mount Revelstoke National Park at Revelstoke.

Past Revelstoke the Monashee Mountains have to be traversed. The road finally descends south past Shuswap Lake to Kamloops, in the wild valley of the Thompson River.

Kamloops–
Vancouver
(433 km (269 mi.))

From Kamloops the road descends along the valley of the Thompson River to Cache Creek, where the river turns south before the Cascade Range. At Lytton about 1½ hours by car downstream the Thompson River joins the Fraser River, flowing fast from the north. A breathtaking road leads down to the Fraser Valley to Vancouver on the Pacific coast.

Plenty of time should be allowed to visit the city of Vancouver. There are numerous memorable excursions to be made from here: Victoria on Vancouver Island, the Inside Passage, a steam train journey to Squamish and a car journey to Whistler, and not least a visit into the neighbouring United States where Seattle and the Olympic National Park are within easy reach.

Montréal to Thunder Bay

Montréal–Toronto
(about 500 km
(310 mi.))

From Montréal take the Macdonald Parkway (motorway; Highway Nr. 401) in a south-westerly direction along the Saint Lawrence Seaway to Kingston allowing time to visit this town. It is also possible to visit the area around the St Lawrence Islands (Thousand Island) National Park (Kingston).

From here continue along the northern bank of Lake Ontario, past the pretty, little towns of Cobourg and Oshawa, to Toronto. It is worth spending a few days in the provincial capital and also making a detour to Kitchener–Waterloo and the region where the Mennonites live. More spectacular is the trip from Toronto to the Niagara Falls, situated between Lake Ontario and Lake Erie. It passes the industrial town of Hamilton and crosses the Welland Channel.

Toronto–Sudbury
(375 km (233 mi.))

Leave Toronto on Highway 400 heading north. After just 100 km it comes to Lake Simcoe and the town of Barrie, followed by the charming little town Orillia. It proceeds north-west to the south-east tip of Georgian Bay, part of Lake Huron. The small town of Midland and St Mary-among-the-Hurons National Site (rebuilt mission station and large pilgrimage church) can be seen here.

From St Mary-among-the-Hurons proceed north through the popular recreation area "Muskoka", a "land of thousand lakes and islands". National road Nr. 69 runs parallel to the eastern bank of Georgian Bay north to the mining town of Sudbury, where the largest nickel mine in the world is situated.

From Sudbury a 130 km (81 mi.) stretch crosses east to North Bay (see above).

From Sudbury national road Nr. 17 leads west to the North Channel of Lake Huron and passes areas of natural beauty before coming to the port and lock town Sault Ste Marie, Ontario. A visit to the locks leading to the Upper Lake is essential. Time permitting an excursion on the Algoma Railway into the imposing mountain countryside north of Sault Ste Marie is recommended.

Sudbury–Sault
Ste Mary
(552 km (343 mi.))

From Sault Ste Marie follow the east bank of the Upper Lake, through Lake Superior Park to Wawa. Further north is the town of White River from where the Pukaskwa National Park can be visited to the west.

The main route (route Nr.17) continues past Marathon and Terrace Bay on the north coast of the Upper Lake to Nipigon where it rejoins the TransCanada Highway and comes to Thunder Bay.

Sault Ste Marie–
Thunder Bay
(595 km (370 mi.))

Calgary to Kamloops

From Calgary express road Nr. 2 leads north to Edmonton. There is much to see in the provincial capital of Alberta. Time permitting an excursion from Edmonton north to the Lesser Slave Lake and the Pelican Mountains is recommended, as is a visit to the Northern Woods and Water Route in the north of Alberta.

Calgary–
Edmonton
(300 km (186 mi.))

From Edmonton the Yellowhead Highway (national road Nr. 16) heads west to the Rocky Mountains. Passing the towns of Edson and Hinton it reaches the valley of the Athabasca River. Proceed upstream to the Jasper National Park with the recreation area of the same name.

From Jasper the 287 km (178 mi.)-long panoramic Icefields Parkway leads south along a long valley, crossed by steps and barriers, to Banff, to rejoin the above mentioned route.

Edmonton–
Jasper
(360 km (223 mi.))

From Jasper the route crosses Yellowhead Pass into the upper Fraser Valley near Valemont. From here Highway Nr. 5 leads over another pass southwards into the valley of the North Thompson River finally reaching Clearwater and Kamloops, the destination of this stage.

Jasper–Kamloops
(430 km (272 mi.))

Medicine Hat to Vancouver

A southern variation on the route, the "Crowsnest Highway", runs from Medicine Hat, Alberta, more or less parallel to the Canadian/US border westwards to the Pacific coast

The Crowsnest Highway (national road Nr. 3) runs from Medicine Hat westwards through the southern Canadian prairie. Via Lethbridge and Fort MacLeod it leads to the Rocky Mountains, where the first major incline is negotiated by Crowsnest Pass.

To the south of the pass the Waterton-Glacier International Peace Park extends over the border. It is well worth a visit and comprises the Waterton Lakes National Park and the US Glacier National Park.

Medicine Hat–
Cranbrooke
(480 km (298 mi.))

From Cranbrook follow the Crowsnest Highway (national road Nr, 95) south-west as far as Erickson and Creston. North of Creston the winding Kootenay Lake is worth a detour.

From Creston the routes closely follows the Canadian-US border and continues to Trail.

Cranbrooke-Trail
(236 km (147 mi.))

Round Tours by Car

Trail–Osoyoos (227 km (141 mi.))	Not far north from Trail, near Castlegar, the Crowsnest Highway (now national road Nr. 3) turns south-west and comes to the border town Grand Fork (from here a road leads to Spokane in Washington, USA). The Crowsnest Highway heads west along the border Osoyoos in the Okanagan Valley.
Osyoos– Vancouver (403 km (250 mi.))	West of Osoyoos, still on road Nr. 3, it crosses the high upland mountains of the Cascade Range and descends into the Fraser Valley near Hope. It continues descending down the Fraser Valley to Vancouver on the Pacific coast.

Round Tours by Car

Distances given are approximate

Atlantic provinces

Nova Scotia, Prince Edward Island	Round trip (2–3 weeks; 2000 km (1243 mi.)): Halifax–Lunenburg–Yarmouth–Annapolis Valley–Amherst–Cape Tormentine/New Brunswick-by ferry to Borden, Prince Edward Island (¾ hour)–Charlottetown (possible day tours of Canada's smallest province)–Wood Islands–return by ferry to Caribou, Nova Scotia (1½ hours)–Cape Breton Island–Cabot Trail–Sydney–Louisburg–Port Hastings–Halifax.
Nova Scotia, New Brunswick, Prince Edward Island, Newfoundland	Round trip (4 weeks; 3100 km (1926 mi.) without the ferry crossings): Halifax–Lunenburg–Liverpool–Digby–by ferry to Saint John, (New Brunswick; 2–3 hours)–St Andrews–Fredericton–Moncton–Cape Tormentine–by ferry to Borden, Prince Edward Island (¾ hour)–Summerside–Cavendish–Charlottetown–Wood Islands–by ferry to Caribou, Nova Scotia (1½ hours)–Baddeck–Cabot Trail–Sydney–Louisburg–North Sydney–by ferry to Port-aux-Basques (Newfoundland; 6 hours)–Cornerbrook–Gander–St John's (through Terra Nova National Park)–Argentia by ferry to North Sydney, Nova Scotia (18 hours)–Port Hastings–Sherbrooke–Halifax.

Québec

Montréal–Québec	Round trip (1 week; 1100 km (683 mi.)): Montréal–Trois Rivières–Québec (city)–visit to Île d'Orleans–return via Québec along the south side of the St Lawrence River to Montréal.
Québec– St Laurent– Gaspésie	Round trip (2 weeks; 2000 km (1243 mi.) without the ferry): Québec (city)–St Foy–Charry–Montmagny–Ste-Jean-Port-Joli–Rivière-du-Loup–Trois-Pistoles–Rimouski–Grand-Métis–Matane–Cap-Chat–Forillon National Park–Gaspé–Percé–Port-Daniel–Bonaventure–Carleton–Oak-Bay–Mann Settlement–Causapscal–Sayabec–Ste Angèle-de-Merci–Ste Flavie–Rimouski–Trois-Pistoles–Rivière-du-Loup–by ferry to Saint-Siméon (1¼ hours)–La Malbaie–Clermont–St-Tite-des-Caps–St-Anne-de-Beaupré–Québec.

Ontario

Ontario I	Round trip (1 week; 1000 km (621 mi.)): Toronto–Midland–St Mary-among-the-Hurons–Muskoka region–Huntsville–Algonquin National Park–Ottawa–Kingston–Upper Canada Village–Toronto.

Round trip (1 week; 1000 km (621 mi.)):
Toronto–Midland–Muskoka Region–Huntsville–North Bay–on the TransCanada Highway to Ottawa–Kingston–Upper Canada Village–Toronto.

Ontario II

Round trip (1–2 weeks; 2200 km (1367 mi.)):
Toronto–Hamilton–St Catherines–Niagara on the Lake–Niagara Falls–Brandford–Guelph–Kitchener-Waterloo–Stratford–London–Point Pelee–Windsor–Chatham–Sarnia–Ipperwash–Pinery–Southampton–Owen Sound–Tobermorey–Manitoulin–Sudbury–Parry Sound–Wasaga Beach–Toronto.

Ontario III

Round trip (5–6 weeks; 6300 km (3937 mi.)):
Toronto–Hamilton–St Catherines–Niagara on the Lake–Niagara Falls–Brantford–Kitchener–Waterloo–Stratford–London–Point Pelee–Leamington–Amhersburg, Windsor–Chatham–Sarnia–Ipperwash–Pinery–Southampton–Owen Sound–Tovermorey–Manitoulin–Sault St Marie–Wawa–Thunderbay–Fort Francis–Lake of the Woods–Kenora–Dryden–Thunderbay–Hearst–Cochrane–Iroquois Falls–North Bay–Huntsville–Barry's Bay–Pembroke–Ottawa–Morrisburg–Brockville–Kingston–Belleville–Toronto.

Ontario IV

Manitoba, Saskatchewan

Round trip (2 weeks; 2000 km (1243 mi.)):
Winnipeg–Brandon–Regina–Saskatoon–Prince Albert National Park–Yorkton–Dauphin–Portage la Prairie–Winnipeg.

Manitoba, Saskatchewan I

Round trip (2–3 weeks; 2500 km (1553 mi.)):
Winnipeg–Flin Flon–The Pas (through Grass River and Clearwater Parks)–Prince Albert, Saskatchewan–Regina–Yorkton–Dauphin–Winnipeg.

Manitoba, Saskatchewan II

Round trip (2–3 weeks; 2500 km (1553 mi.)):
Winnipeg–Portage la Prairie–Dauphin–Clear Lake (through Riding Mountain National Park)–Brandon–Regina–Moose Law–Prince Albert Waskesiu Lake in Prince Albert National Park–Saskatoon–Yorkton–Winnipeg.

Manitoba, Saskatchewan III

West Canada

Round trip (1 week; 1100 km (683 mi.)):
Calgary–Banff–Jasper–Edmonton–Calgary.

Rocky Mountains

Round trip (3–5 weeks; 2500 km (1553 mi.) without ferry crossings)
From Edmonton to Dawson Creek, the start of the Yukon-Alaska Highway, Whitehorse–Fairbanks–Haines Junction-Haines, Alaska, by the Alaska State Ferry to Prince Rupert–from there by ferry to Port Hardy, Vancouver Island (31 hours)–Vancouver.

Yukon–Alaska Highway

Alternative (2100 km (1304 mi.)):
Prince Rupert–land route to Prince George–Williams Lake–Cache Creek–Jasper–Edmonton (2100 km).

Round trip (3–4 weeks; 3000 km (1864 mi.)):
Vancouver–Okanagan Valley–Rogers Pass–Glacier National Park–Emerald Lake–Lake Louise–Banff–Columbia Icefield–Jasper–Prince George–Clinton–Vancouver.

British Columbia, Alberta I

Round trip (3–4 weeks; 3000 km (1864 mi.) without ferry crossings):
Calgary–Banff–Lake Louise–Yoho National Park–Golden/Glacier National

British Columbia, Alberta II

Park–Revelstoke National Park-Shuswap Lake–Okanagan Valley (Vernon–Kelowna–Penticton) Princeton–Manning Provincial Park–Hope–Vancouver–car ferry to Victoria (1 hour 40 mins.)–Duncan–Nanaimo–Courtnay Cumberland–Strathcona Provincial Park–Campbell River–Port McNeill–Port Hardy–car ferry to Prince Rupert (18 hours, must be booked in advance!); from Prince Rupert on the Yellowhead Highway to Terrace–Smithers–Houston–Burns Lake–Fraser Lake (Fort Fraser)–Vanderhoof–Prince of George–Mount Robson Provincial Park–Jasper–Columbia Glacier–Banff–Calgary.

Cariboo-Rocky Mountains

Round trip (3–4 weeks; 3000 km (1864 mi.)):
From Vancouver on the TransCanada Highway along the Fraser River to Lillooet. Proceed along the trail of the gold diggers and trappers to the 100 Mile House, in the direction of Quesnel. Here there is an interesting detour to the ghost town of Barkerville and to the Bowron Lake Park. Continue to Prince George–Jasper National Park–Banff National Park–Lake Louise–Banff–Kootenay National Park–return along the TransCanada Highway through the Yoho National Park-Glacier National Park–Rogers Pass–Okanagan Valley–Vancouver.

Totem–Circular tour

Round trip (3–4 weeks; 2800 km 1738 mi.)):
Vancouver–Penticton–Banff–Jasper–Prince George–Prince Rupert–by ferry back to Port Hardy Vancouver Island (18 hours)–Vancouver.

Rail Journeys

VIA Rail

Although the railway plays an ever diminishing role in passenger transport, Canada's vast territory can still be "experienced" by rail. The network used by VIA Rail extends from Halifax on the Atlantic coast of Nova Scotia, to Vancouver and Prince Rupert on the Pacific coast of British Columbia. 14,000 km (8700 mi.) of track link more then 400 cities, towns and smaller communities.

Forming the backbone of the Canadian rail network are the transcontinental lines of the privately owned Canadian Pacific (CP) and state owned Canadian National (CN), on which the operating company VIA Rail now run their transcontinental expresses.

The train journey across the continent, from the tidal Atlantic coast, via the great cities of the St Lawrence lowlands and raw landscape of the Canadian Shield, to the wide-open spaces of the prairies and mountain ranges of the Cordilleras, is one of the most fantastic in the world.

Careful planning essential

Crossing Canada by train needs careful planning however. There is not the flexibility offered by coach companies operating transcontinental services. Rail services being more restricted, reservations must be made and a rail pass is of less obvious value. A further disadvantage is that some exceptionally beautiful countryside is crossed at night, a big disappointment in the case of the Cordilleras in particular.

Express services (selection)

"The Ocean"

"The Ocean" express makes the journey from Halifax (Nova Scotia) to Montréal (Québec) several times a week. Taking barely 21 hours, it follows the coastline of New Brunswick and the St Lawrence valley to Québec (1350 km (839 mi.)), traversing the most varied of landscapes. Adjacent areas of interest such as the Gaspé Peninsula, Prince Edward Island and even Newfoundland, are accessible either by bus or ferry and bus connection.

Leaving Halifax the train proceeds via Truro and Amherst to Moncton (New Brunswick), then up the east coast of New Brunswick and on via Miramichi, Bathurst and Campbellton to Matapédia on the scenically delightful Gaspé Peninsula in Québec province. Descending to the St Lawrence River, it makes its way along the river's southern bank via Rimouski and Rivière-du-Loup to Lévis, a suburb of Québec City situated across the river from the picturesque Old Town. The final leg of the journey to Montréal follows the increasingly narrow St Lawrence southwestwards via Drummundville to St-Lambert.

The section over the St Lawrence plain to Montréal, a city rich in tradition and the second largest French-speaking city in the world, is relatively monotonous.

The second most popular express train in the Canadian east is "Le Chaleur", commuting between Montréal and the Gaspé Peninsula. It follows the same route as "The Ocean" from Montréal to Campbellton (New Brunswick), before branching off north along the beautiful southern coast of the Gaspé Peninsula to its terminus at Percé.

"Le Chaleur"

The communications "corridor" extending from Québec on the St Lawrence River in the north-east, to Windsor in the extreme south-west of Ontario province, comprises the most densely populated area of Canada. The backbone of the corridor is the St Lawrence River and lakes Ontario and Erie along which are situated some of the country's oldest and largest cities, i.e. in addition to Québec city, Montréal, Ottawa and Toronto, as well as the world-famous Niagara Falls. Numerous LRC trains (L = light, R = rapid and C = comfortable) ply the corridor daily, the most travelled routes being: Toronto–Kingston–Ottawa; Toronto–Kingston–Montréal; Ottawa–Montréal; Montréal–Québec; Toronto–Niagara Falls; Toronto–London–Windsor.

Corridor services

The flagship of Canada's railways is "The Canadian", a thrice weekly express service from Toronto to Vancouver and back. The journey of some 4500 km (2796 mi.) is completed in three days and three nights. From Toronto the train heads north-west through the seemingly endless forests of Ontario via Sudbury to the prairie town of Winnipeg.

"The Canadian"

The journey across Canada aboard the "Canadian" on its historically fascinating and spectacularly scenic route, remains an overwhelming experience. On such a journey the contrast between the densely populated Anglo-Canadian cultural landscape of Lake Ontario, and the untamed wildness of the Canadian Shield where the mining country around Sudbury is typical of many mining towns in north Ontario, is very marked. Beyond Kenora there is a sudden transition in scenery from the rugged hills of the Canadian Shield to the flat agricultural plain near the former Lake Agassiz, before the train at last reaches Winnipeg. A stopover in this intriguing city should definitely include visits to the Museum of Man and Nature, the old cultural centre of St Boniface, and the neighbouring Mennonite settlements.

A stretch of flat, monotonous country leads on to Saskatoon, a town of many bridges with a European feel. Next comes a belt of park-like scenery on the edge of the prairies, then the prairies themselves, a landscape of vast farms and massive grain elevators, the "cathedrals of the prairies". Edmonton, capital of Alberta, stands high above the North Saskatchewan River and justifies a stopover of one or more days, in particular on account of its Legislature Building and newly redeveloped government quarter, the modern high-rise architecture of its city centre, the old Fort Edmonton and – in stark contrast – the world's biggest and most modern shopping mall.

Ahead on the next stage of the journey lie the Rocky Mountains and the magnificent Jasper National Park. Jasper on the CN line, together with Banff on the CP line further south, is the most popular tourist destination in the Rocky Mountains. Continuing, there is a panoramic view of Mount Robson (3954 m (12,977 ft)), the highest summit in this section of the Rockies, before the descent through the impressive gorges of the

Rail Journeys

Thompson and Fraser rivers on the final lap of the journey to Vancouver on the Pacific coast of British Columbia.

The "Canadian" is made up of carriages from the legendary "Silver and Blue Class" trains. Manufactured originally in the 1950s, these offer the ultimate in luxury, a virtual hotel on wheels. There are comfortable sleepers and couchettes with showers and toilets, as well as saloon and dining-cars. Each train is equipped with two "dome cars" affording superb all-round vistas of the scenic grandeur.

"The Skeena"

"The Skeena" express runs thrice weekly on the 1160 km (720 mi.) route between Jasper and the Pacific coast port of Prince Rupert, the two-day journey including an overnight stop in the town of Prince George. The Skeena's dome car ensures splendid views of the magnificent high mountain scenery of this part of central British Columbia.

The Malahat

Scenically equally varied but much shorter is the 225 km (139 mi.) trip along the east coast of Vancouver Island (British Columbia), from the capital Victoria to Nanaimo and Courtenay. There are regular ferry services to the mainland (B.C. Ferries to Vancouver or Prince Rupert).

Hudson Bay

A completely different experience is to be had on the 1697 km (1054 mi.)-long Hudson Bay Line which runs from Winnipeg to Churchill through forests, bogs and tundra and over permafrost, normally taking about 35 hours. Any delays due to the weather are made bearable by the comfortable provision (sleeping and dining cars).

B.C. Railway, Cariboo Prospector, Royal Hudson

In addition to the long-distance trains already mentioned – without exception operated by VIA Rail on Canadian Pacific (CP) or Canadian National (CN) routes – there are several private railways of tourist interest. The first is the scenic and technically remarkable 742 km (461 mi.)-long line of the British Columbia Railway from Prince George to North Vancouver. A historic steam train drawn by the legendary "Royal Hudson 2860" engine, plies the 61 km (40 mi.) southern section along Howe Sound (Vancouver–Squamish) daily in summer, a journey of about two hours.

"Rocky Mountaineer"

The luxuriously appointed, privately owned "Rocky Mountaineer" runs between Calgary (or Jasper) and Vancouver. Leaving Calgary, the rich Alberta oil town with its modern skyline, the train heads westward on the historic Canadian Pacific line, to be abruptly confronted by the soaring mountain wall of the Rockies. At Canmore, providing the weather is good, there is a fine view of the snow-capped "Three Sisters". Soon afterwards the popular winter (arid summer) resort of Banff is reached. Other highlights on this mountainous section with peaks up to 3600 m (11,815 ft) are Lake Louise, the Kicking Horse Pass, the two famous spiral tunnels, and the Rogers Pass through the Selkirk Mountains with its two long tunnels – the 9 km (5½ mi.) Connaught Tunnel, completed in 1916, and the almost 15 km (9½ mi.) Mount McDonald Tunnel and magnificent 94 m (308 ft)-high Stoney Creek Bridge. The next lap of the journey is across the dry, warm Kamloops basin, enjoying an almost Mediterranean feel, and through the rugged gorges of the Thompson and Friseur rivers to Yale. The final 100 km (60 mi.) follows the well-cultivated Fraser valley to Vancouver.

The Jasper-bound section of the "Rocky Mountaineer" takes the route north from Kamloops into the Rockies, passing Mount Robson on its way to and from Jasper.

Algoma Central Railway

The Algoma Central Railway offers a 183 km (114 mi.) excursion through the Algoma Wilderness to the Agawa Canyon north of Sault Ste Marie. This is extremely popular, especially in autumn when the leaves are turning colour.

One of the more unusual railway experiences is provided by the 300 km (186 mi.) journey on the Ontario Northland Railway from Cochrane to Moosonee, a historic fur-trading station on James Bay (on the Hudson Bay). Quite apart from the rugged, bog-ridden landscape, the passengers on the "Polar Bear Express" – Indians, trappers and adventurers – are an experience in themselves.

Ontario Northland Railway, Polar Bear Express

From Skagway (Alaska), at the northern end of the Inside Passage, a narrow-gauge railway climbs a historic stretch to White Pass and the station at Fraser, the small town at the north-western extremity of British Columbia. From here a bus can be taken to Whitehorse, capital of the Yukon Territory.

White Pass & Yukon Railway

Railway enthusiasts can enjoy a wide range of journeys by steam. In addition to the "Royal Hudson" (North Vancouver–Howe Sound–Squamish; see above), steam trains operate in Calgary (Heritage Park), Edmonton (Fort Edmonton), Winnipeg (Prairie Dog), Ottawa (Gatineau Park) and around Stettler (Alberta).

Museum trains

The passenger services operated by VIA Rail and other rail companies are restricted to more or less profitable routes. However buses extend access to the hinterland from nearly all stations of any size. Bus timetables are co-ordinated with train arrival and departure times.

Bus–rail combinations

Coach Tours

Canada can be explored relatively inexpensively by coach. Many companies offer packages, anything from short breaks of just a few days to extended trips lasting several weeks. In addition so-called Inter City Buses operate between Canada's main centres, allowing transcontinental travel in either direction (Inter City Bus departure points are usually conveniently situated in city and town centres).

Canadian coaches are generally comfortable, with air-conditioning and onboard toilets. There is often more leg room than is usual on European coaches.

Greyhound Canada offers the greatest range of services between Ontario and the Canadian West, with offices in all the larger towns. Other companies operate province to province or region to region.

Ontario–Western Canada

The Calgary area and the Rocky Mountain National Parks most popular with tourists (Banff National Park, Jasper National Park, Yoho National Park) are well served by coaches owned by the "Brewster" company.

Rocky Mountains

"Voyageur" coaches operate on all major routes in the adjacent provinces of Ontario and Québec.

Ontario–Québec

"SMT Eastern" buses provide services in the provinces of New Brunswick and Prince Edward Island. Acadian Lines serves Nova Scotia.

Atlantic Canada

Advice | The following selected places to visit are arranged in alphabetical order. English and French are the official languages used in Canada. Each place is shown in the form normally used locally; the English name is used in those regions where English is the main language, and French spellings in the French-speaking areas.

Abbotsford · Clearbrook H 6

Province: British Columbia. Population: 106,000

Information | Abbotsford Chamber of Commerce, 2462 McCallum Rd, Abbotsford, BC V2S 3P9; tel. (604) 8599651.

Location | Abbotsford and Clearbrook, two parishes which have grown together and now number over 100,000 inhabitants, lie in the shadow of the 3285 m (10,780 ft) high Mount Baker which forms part of the Cascade Range of mountains south of the state border. These two towns form the centre of the Fraser Valley, where the mild climate has led to its development as an agricultural region, which, for example, produces more than 80 per cent of Canada's raspberry crop.

Events | The high point of the year is the Abbotsford Berry Festival held every June. As well as fields of fruit bushes and narcissi – the latter being a magnificent sight in spring – large chicken farms also dominate the landscape; some 80 per cent of British Columbia's eggs are produced in this region. Every August the Abbotsford International Air Show, one of the largest of its kind in North America, is held here.

Matsqui-Sumas-Museum | The Matsqui-Sumas-Abbotsford Museum, housed in Tretheway House, 2313 Ware St., which was built in 1919 and has recently been lovingly restored, is rather out of the ordinary and offers the opportunity to study exhibits of items used by the Red Indians who originally inhabited the country as well as memorabilia from the pioneering period. Particularly interesting are the documents about Sumas Lake, which was drained in 1924, thus producing 12,140 ha (30,000 acres) of fertile grazing and farmland which lie almost one metre below sea-level and are protected by means of a dyke from the risk of being flooded by the Fraser River. Open Mon.–Sat. 10am–noon, 1pm–4pm.

Mennonite Historical Society Museum | The Museum of the Mennonite Historical Society of British Columbia will be found in the Clearbrook Community Centre at 2825 Clearbrook Road. It provides information about the history and life-style of the Mennonites in British Columbia. Open Mon.–Fri. 9am–4.30pm, Sat. 9am–noon.

Acadia H 17/18

Provinces: New Brunswick, Nova Scotia, Prince Edward Island, Québec

Information | Tourist information offices in the above provinces.

Location | The areas south-east of the Lower St Lawrence River and on the Bay of Fundy, once called New France, are now known as "Acadia". Many sections of this land which has been developed by man over the centuries now

◀ *Vancouver skyline*

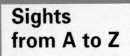

**Sights
from A to Z**

Automats are a convenient source of stamps in many towns, being found particularly at airports, bus and train stations, and newspaper kiosks. But they only sell stamps for use within Canada.

Stamp automats

The current cost of a stamp for a letter under 20 g. or a standard postcard to Europe is 95 cents (46 cents within Canada, 55 cents to USA).

Mail to Europe

Canadian post offices will keep mail marked "General Delivery", as poste restante, up to 15 days, after which, if not collected, it will be returned to sender. Letters should be addressed to the recipient c/o General Delivery, Main Post Office, then the name of the town, the province, Canada and postcode.

General delivery/
poste restante

Public Holidays

A number of Canada's public holidays are taken on a particular Monday in the month or the nearest Monday to the date in question so that Canadians get several long weekends during the year.

The same applies to some of the public holidays that are celebrated only by certain provinces.

National holidays

New Year: January 1st

Good Friday and Easter Monday: March/April

Victoria Day: Monday before May 25th

Canada Day: July 1st

Labour Day: 1st Monday in September

Thanksgiving: 2nd Monday in October

Remembrance Day: November 11th

Christmas Day and Boxing Day: December 25th/26th

Provincial holidays

St. Patrick's Day (Newfoundland & Labrador): March 17th or Monday before

St. George's Day (Newfoundland & Labrador): April 23rd or Monday before

St-Jean Baptiste (La Fête Nationale) (St John the Baptist, Québec): June 24th

Discovery Day, St John's Day (Newfoundland & Labrador): Monday nearest to June 25th

Memorial Day (Newfoundland): Beginning of July

Orangeman's Day (Newfoundland & Labrador): Monday nearest to July 10th

Heritage Day (Alberta)
British Columbia Day (British Columbia)
New Brunswick Day (New Brunswick)
Civic Holiday (Manitoba, Northwest Territories, Ontario, Saskatchewan): 1st Monday in August

Discovery Day (Yukon): 3rd Monday in August

Public Transport

Canada has a good public transport system. Buses operate on scheduled routes in all the main built-up areas, and in the major cities the local transport network is particularly close-knit. Toronto and Montréal have underground (subway), systems, while Calgary, Edmonton and Vancouver have light rail transit (LRT) mass transportation systems.

Fares

Compared with Europe fares in most Canadian cities are relatively cheap. Usually the exact money has to be given – bus drivers don't sell tickets manually or carry any change.

City tours

Every Canadian city has guided bus tours and local excursions. Details from travel agents, hotel reception, or the local tourist information centre.

Radio and Television

Canada has broadcasting to suit every taste, from the bilingual radio and TV broadcasts of the Canadian Broadcasting Corporation to innumerable local stations, as well as American network television.

Radio

AM and FM radio stations carry on round the clock, transmitting news, music, sport, etc. put out by CBC and local and national independents.

Television

Canadian TV uses the NTSC system, not PAL or SECAM as in Europe, so anyone wanting to play videotapes from Europe could encounter problems.

There are TV sets in almost every hotel room. The public service stations are free, but other channels are "Pay TV", so have to be paid for.

Rail Travel

Canrail pass

VIA Rail's Canrail pass, which must be purchased prior to departure for Canada, offers unlimited coach class travel for up to 30 consecutive days.

Concessionary fares

Children under the age of two accompanied by an adult travel free; those aged 2 to 11 pay half fare. For the over 60s there is a reduction of 10 per cent. No reductions on the cost of sleepers or couchettes.

VIA Rail

VIA Rail was set up as a Crown Corporation in 1978 to act as Canada's national passenger train service, although the rails and rolling stock still belong to the former rail companies. It has to cover its costs, and was forced to limit its operations considerably in 1990 by such factors as competition from the airlines. Concentrating on passenger comfort and good service delivery, it continues to operate a number of routes in eastern Canada, including Québec/Montréal, Montréal/Ottawa, Montréal/Toronto, Ottawa/Toronto, Toronto/Niagara Falls and Toronto/Windsor. Passenger services also operate out of Vancouver and Prince Rupert over the Rockies to Edmonton and from Winnipeg to Churchill on

Hudson Bay. A high-speed stretch is planned for Montréal/Toronto to take advantage of the increased use, but it has to be said that ultimately the income from passenger travel is only a fraction of that earned from carrying freight.

There are some regional carriers around the main cities who use part of the rail network for passenger services, and are subsidised by the provincial and local authorities in question.

> Regional
> passenger trains

Several provinces, such as Ontario, also maintain rail lines for economic and social purposes.

Since most of Canada's rail system, apart from in the Rockies and around the major cities, is single-track, while Canadian freight-trains are longer, heavier, and slower than those in Europe, passenger trains and scenic railtours often have to be shunted into sidings to wait for freight to pass, causing considerable delays. The Canadian rail corporations are also not good at ploughing their quite considerable profits back into the system.

> Delays

VIA Rail Canada Inc., C.P.8116, 2 place Ville-Marie, Montréal, Québec H3B 2C9

> Rail carriers

Algoma Central Railway, 129 Bay Street, PO Box 7000, Sault Ste Marie, Ontario P6A 5P6

Amtrak National Railroad Passenger Corporation, 50 Massachusetts Avenue NE, Washington, D.C. 20002, USA

British Columbia Rail Ltd., PO Box 2790, Vancouver, British Columbia V6B 3X2

Ontario Northland Railway, 65 Front Street W, Toronto, Ontario M5J 1E6

The flagship of the Silver and Blue class trains of VIA Rail is the "Canadian" which operates on the stretch Toronto–Winnipeg–Edmonton–Jasper–Vancouver. The silver-blue luxury trains of the 50s with their high-quality decorated rolling stock of shining aluminium, particularly the "Dome Car" and "Park Car", are soon to be re-polished. In five days passengers travel in the highest comfort from Lake Ontario to the Pacific and get to know a little about the beautiful and interesting countryside. The "Skeena" takes two days from Jasper in the Rocky Mountains to Prince Rupert on the Pacific Coast. In eastern Canada the comfortable "Chaleur" connects Montréal with the Gaspé Peninsula, and the "Ocean" which connects Montréal to Halifax.

> Luxury Trains

Also popular is the "Rocky Mountaineer" belonging to the private Great Canadian Railtour Company. This tourist train operates three times a week during the high season on the line Vancouver–Banff–Calgary and Vancouver–Kamloops–Jasper. Further information from: Rocky Mountaineer Railtours, 1150 Station Street, 1st floor, Vancouver, BC, Canada V6A 2X7; tel. (604) 606 7245, fax (604) 606 7250.

See also Facts and Figures, Canada by Rail

Ranch and Farm Holidays

Holidays on a ranch or farm are rapidly increasing in popularity. Accommodation can range from small, simple farms to the most splendid of ranches, where there are opportunities for horseback riding, fishing, sailing and canoeing, not to mention golf in some cases. Further details can be obtained from travel agents.

Rail Transport
Passenger Services
of VIA Rail

	Via Rail
	Other Bus Services
	British Columbia Railway
	Algoma Central
	Ontario Northland
	Limited service
	Amtrak
......	Ferries

St John's
Gander
Corner Brook
Ardentia
Port-aux-Basques
Gaspé
Percé
North Sydney
Mont-Joli
Matapédia
Sydney
Jonquière
Campbellton
Moosonee
Edmundston
Borden
Charlottetown
Cochrane
Hervey
Rivière-
Fredericton
Hearst
Senneterre
Rivière-
du-Loup
Truro
Kapuskasing
Val d'Or
Québec
Levis
Halifax
Rouyn-Noranda
Trois-
Rivières
Bar
Harbour
Moncton
Caureol
Trois-
Digby
White River
Rivières
Ottawa
Sherbrooke
Yarmouth
under Bay
Sudbury
North Bay
Montréal
Saint John
Sault Ste. Marie
Havelock
Brockville
Kitchener
Toronto
Kingston
Stratford
Niagara Falls
Sarnia
Hamilton
London
New York
Chicago
Windsor
Detroit

609

Restaurants

Eating out in Canada covers the whole spectrum from fast-food outlets to gourmet restaurants, and reflects the ethnic diversity of the Canadian people. Salmon, lobster, steak and other national delights can be found on the menu of every quality establishment, as well as a variety of more exotic dishes depending on where the chef comes from.

Canada's individual regions have their own specialities (see Food and Drink), so a visit to a restaurant can be an excursion into the culinary unknown. Montréal is traditionally the country's gastronomic capital, owing to its French cuisine, while the four Maritime provinces – Newfoundland, Prince Edward Island, New Brunswick and Nova Scotia – specialise in seafood, especially lobster. Toronto ranks third for good food on the east coast. Although here too there is a strong French influence, a great many other ethnic groups are represented among its restauranteurs. In Manitoba, Saskatchewan and Alberta good hearty meals are served, often with a flavour of the Ukraine. On the West Coast there is superb fish and seafood, while the best gastronomic choice is to be had in Vancouver and Victoria, from a international cuisine and regional specialities.

Tax

Sales tax, at varying rates, is charged on food in restaurants in almost all Canada's provinces.

Alcoholic drinks

Alcoholic drinks are only available in establishments with the appropriate licence. This means going without a beer in many fast-food eating places, or often finding that it is only possible to get a drink with a meal during certain hours.

The following list of restaurants is clearly only a selection, listed in alphabetical order by province or territory. The Hotels section also includes a number of restaurants.

Abbreviations

L = Luxury restaurants
M/L = High standard restaurants
M = Medium standard restaurants
M/B = Good inexpensive restaurants
B = Budget restaurants

Alberta

Banff National Park

Buffalo Mountain Lodge, about a mile west of Banff on Tunnel Mountain; tel. (403) 7622400
The Lodge restaurant is currently reckoned to be the best (and most expensive) in Banff; very good beef and lamb but also excellent local trout and Pacific salmon.

Coyote's, 206 Caribou Street, Banff; tel. (403) 7623963
Open daily 7.30am to 10pm. The food at Coyote's is good and relatively cheap; besides popular American south-west type dishes there are also tasty vegetarian specials.

Calgary

The Conservatory, 209 4th Avenue; tel. (403) 2661980
Open Mon. to Fri. 11.30am to 2pm, plus Mon. to Sat. 5.30 to 10.30pm. Outstanding gourmet restaurant in the Delta Bow Valley Hotel devoted to "la cuisine française".

★Owl's Nest, in the Westin Hotel, 4th Avenue; tel. (403) 2261611
Open 11.30am to 2.30pm and 5.30 to 11pm. Probably the best but also the most expensive restaurant in Calgary; primarily exquisite French cuisine.

The Manor Cafe, 10109 125th Street; tel. (780) 4827577
Open Mon. to Fri. 11.30am to 10pm, Sat., Sun. 5 to 10pm. Good restaurant with extensive menu in attractive surroundings.

Edmonton

Packrat Louie, 10335 83rd Avenue, Old Strathcona; tel. (780) 4330123
Open Mon. to Sat. 11.30am to 11.30pm. Currently by far the best "Italian" in Edmonton, with excellent creations of the "new Italian cuisine" as well as pasta and pizza.

★La Ronde, revolving restaurant in the Crowne Plaza Hotel, 10111 Bellamy Hill; tel. (780) 4286611
Rather over-expensive but worth recommending for its wonderful views and good cuisine.

★Posthotel; tel. (403) 5223989
Open daily 11.30am to 2pm and 5 to 10pm. The Posthotel offers the best Swiss/French cuisine, plus outstanding French wines.

Lake Louise

Walliser Stube, in Château Lake Louse; tel. (403) 5223511
Swiss cheese fondue and raclette against a backdrop of Canadian glaciers – what more could you want!

British Columbia

★Historic 1912 Inn, south of Penticton; tel. (250) 4976868
Open Tue. to Sun. 5.30 to 10pm. Romantic and tastefully decorated restaurant in historic setting; outstanding cuisine with very popular fish dishes, but sadly rather expensive.

Okanagan Valley
Penticton

MV Fintry Queen; tel. (250) 7632780
Lunch and dinner cruises on this old paddleboat on Lake Kelowna are a very special experience; these take place from Jun.–Sep. daily from noon to 3pm for lunch and 7.30 to 9.30pm for dinner. Fish a speciality.

Kelowna

Smile's, 113 Cow Bay Road; tel. (250) 6243072
Open daily 10am to 10pm. This has long been famed for its exceptional fish dishes.

Prince Rupert

The Loft, 346 Campbell Street; tel. (250) 7254241
Open daily 7am to 10pm. Typical west coast dishes (including Pacific salmon) of the best quality and at really reasonable prices.

Tofino

Chin Chin, 1154 Robson Street; tel. (604) 6887338
Mediterranean cusine with Italian charcoal oven and grill on the Pacific.

Vancouver

Ichibanka, 770 Thurlow Street; tel. (604) 6826262
Unusual Japanese restaurant near the hurly burly of Robson Street, where sushi snacks process past diners on a conveyor belt.

Joe Forte's Seafood House, Thurlow Street; tel. (604) 6691940
One of Vancouver's best fish restaurants.

★Kirin Mandarin, 1166 Alberni Street; tel. (604) 6828833
Very good but relatively expensive Chinese restaurant with highly acclaimed fish cuisine.

★Raintree, 375 Water Street; tel. (604) 6885570
Imaginative West Coast specialities feature on the menu of this acclaimed restaurant, also famous for its select wine list.

★The Teahouse (L/M), 7501 Stanley Park Dr.; tel. (604) 6693281
This restaurant in Stanley Park, famous for its French-style fish cuisine, has a lovely view of English Bay.

Top of Vancouver, revolving restaurant, 555 Hastings Street; tel. (604) 6692220
Good international cuisine at quite moderate prices, plus a superb view of Vancouver.

Water Street Café, Gastown, 300 Water Street; tel. (604) 6892832
Excellent fish dishes and specialities with Italian flair; moderate prices.

Victoria

Sooke Harbour House, 1528 Whiffen Spit Road; tel. (250) 6423421
Open daily 6 to 9.30pm. Very expensive but also very good, with excellent fish.

Spinnaker's, 308 Catherine Street; tel. (250) 3862739
Good value restaurant on the waterfront (Westend) with its own brewery; lovely terrace.

Manitoba

Winnipeg

Alycia's, 559 Cathedral Street; tel. (204) 5828789
Open Mon. to Sat. 8am to 8pm. This attractive little place serves delicious Ukrainian cuisine.

Le Beaujolais, 131 Provencher Blvd.; tel. (204) 2376306
Open Mon. to Fri. 11.30am to 2.30 pm, daily 5 to 10pm. The name says it all: here excellent wines accompany outstanding creations of French cuisine, with a certain inclination to the Provençal.

Charterhouse – Rib Room, York & Hargrave Sts.; tel. (204) 9420101
Famous throughout Winnipeg for its wonderful prime ribs and steaks.

★The Velvet Glove, in the Lombard Hotel, 2 Lombard Place; tel. (204) 9856255
Elegant gourmet restaurant with versatile menu which includes Canadian and international specialities.

New Brunswick

Caraquet

Paulin (M/B), 143 Boulevard St-Pierre Ouest; tel. (506) 7279981
Open daily 5.30 to 10pm. Excellent "cuisine acadienne" which mainly uses high quality regional produce.

Moncton

Pastalli's (B), Main Street; tel. (506) 3831050
Good and quite cheap Italian restaurant, offering a broad range of pastas, pizzas, etc.

★Windjammer (L) & L'Auberge (M), in the Hotel Bonséjour, 750 Main Street; tel. (506) 8544344
Both restaurants, in the town's top hotel, have the same chef; the excellent fish cuisine is famous through eastern Canada.

St Andrew's-by-the-Sea

★The Algonquin; tel. (506) 5298823
The hotel is renowned for its gastronomy; fresh Atlantic salmon and lobster are particular specialities of the masterchef.

Billy's Fish Market (B/M), 159 Charlotte Street; tel. (506) 6723474   Saint John
Open daily 11am to 11pm. Very popular fish restaurant, widely known
for its expertise in cooking salmon.

★Turn of the Tide (L), in the Hilton Hotel, 1 Market Square; tel. (506)
6938484
Open Mon. to Sat. 5.30 to 9.30 pm. One of the top places in New
Brunswick, the Turn of the Tide serves excellent fish and memorable
game specialities.

Marshlands Inn (B/M), Bridge Street; tel. (506) 5360170   Sackville
Long known for its very imaginative creations – including vegetarian
dishes – at sensible prices.

Newfoundland

Atlantica Inn (B), St Bride's, on Route 100; tel. (709) 3372860   Cape St Mary's
The owner is an impassioned chef who serves both good plain fare and
sophisticated fish dishes.

Fisherman's Landing (B), Rocky Harbour, on Highway 430; tel. (709)   Gros Morne
4582060   National Park
Open May to Sep. daily 6am to 11pm. Friendly restaurant with remarkably good fish.

Stella's (M/B), 106 Water Street; tel. (709) 7539625   St John's
Open daily noon to 3pm and 6 to 10pm. Delicious vegetarian dishes and
also good fish and chicken with black beans.

★Stone House (M/L), 8 Kenna's Hill; tel. (709) 7532380
Open daily 11.30am to 2.30pm and 5 to 10pm. Elegant restaurant in an
old (1846) stone house; wonderfully cooked fish and also excellent
game.

The Cellar (L), Baird's Cove; tel. (709) 5798900
Open daily 5.30 to 10pm. Very atmospheric cellar restaurant with all
kinds of delicacies on offer; the grilled trout and the mouthwatering
shrimps are highly recommended.

Northwest Territories

L'Atitudes, Center Square Mall; tel. (867) 9207880   Yellowknife
Open daily 7.30am to 10.30pm. Fairly new and very popular bistro-style
restaurant which serves really good food. Here they serve specialities
of the Far North such as caribou with rosemary, and a broad range of
vegetarian dishes.

Wildcat, Willey Road; tel. (867) 8738850
Open daily 10am to 9pm. This timber cabin harks back to the riproaring
days of the pioneers, and is a sight in itself. Seated on benches at the
long tables guests can sample tasty fish from one of the nearby lakes or
perhaps some of the locally caught game.

Nova Scotia

Leo's (B), 222 St George's St; tel. (902) 5327424   Annapolis Royal
Open May to Sep. daily 9am to 3pm and 5.30 to 9pm. Good family
restaurant in one of eastern Canada's oldest buildings.

Restaurants

Antigonish

★Lobster Treat, 241 Post Road; tel. (902) 8635465
Standing above St George's Bay, where the Scottish Highland Games are held in July, this restaurant specialises in lobster and other seafood dishes.

Sunshine Café (M), 343 Main Street; tel. (902) 8635851
Open daily 11am to 11pm. The patron is an expert at French cuisine; fish, meat, dairy products are from select regional producers.

Baddeck

Auberge Giselle, Shore Road; tel. (902) 2952849
This exquisite restaurant is famed far and wide.

Digby

Harbourview Inn (M), Smith's Cove; tel. (902) 2455686
This small but significant restaurant is not far from the famous Bay of Fundy.

Halifax

Crown Restaurant (L), 1990 Barrington Street in Hotel Halifax; tel. (902) 4256700.
Smart city centre (Scotia Square) restaurant.

★Haliburton House (L), 5184 Morris Street; tel. (902) 4200658
Open daily 5.30 to 9pm. One of the best (and most expensive) restaurants in town, particularly known for its exceptional game dishes.

★Upper Deck Restaurant (L), in the Privateer's Warehouse (in the restored historic quarter around the old waterfront); tel. (902) 4221289
Open daily 5.30 to 10pm. Top restaurant with excellent fish cuisine in a historic setting.

Salty's (M), 1869 Lower Water Street; tel. (902) 4236818
Open daily 11.30am to 2.30pm and 5 to 10pm. Friendly restaurant serving exceptional fish dishes, with a lovely view of the old harbour and its historic ships.

Lunenburg

The Old Fish Factory, in the Fisheries Museum; tel. (902) 6343333
Open mid-May to mid-October daily 11am to 9pm. Popular fish restaurant but serves fine steaks too.

Margaree Valley

★Normaway Inn, Egypt Road (nearly 2 miles off the Cabot Trail); tel. (902) 2482987
This gourmet restaurant, with its excellent cuisine, has long been one of the really smart places for dining out.

Oyster Pond

Golden Coast (B), on Highway 7; tel. (902) 8892386
As the name of the town implies this is a place for outstanding fish dishes; the lovely view more than compensates for the rather plain setting.

Ontario

Kingston

Chez Piggy, Princess Street; tel. (613) 5497673
Open daily 11.30am to midnight. Here you can enjoy imaginative creations – ranging from grilled lamb to Thai beef salad – at acceptable prices.

Niagara
Niagara Falls

Skylon Tower, 5200 Robinson Street; tel. (905) 3562651
Revolving restaurant with magnificent views, good Canadian cuisine and a relatively cheap buffet.

The Buttery, 19 Queen Street; tel. (905) 4682564
Long-established and hence well patronised restaurant in central location.

Royals, in Prince of Wales Hotel, 6 Picton Street; tel. (905) 4683246
Elegant restaurant in historic setting with French élan.

★Le Café, in the National Arts Centre; tel. (613) 5945127
Open 11.30am to midnight. This very civilized restaurant offers exceptionally well-prepared Canadian specialities, especially game and fish, as well as excellent Canadian wines – there is a wonderful view from the terrace of the Rideau Canal.

★Wilfrid's, in the Château Laurier, 1 Rideau Street; tel. (613) 2411414
The elegant restaurant in this grand hotel is most frequented in the evening; its cuisine is exemplary.

Clair de Lune, 81B Clarence Street; tel. (613) 2412200
Open daily 11.30am to 2.30pm and 6 to 11pm. Highly recommended restaurant with French cuisine, and one of the many places to eat in Byward Market.

Acqua, 181 Bay Street; tel. (416) 3687171
Open Mon. to Fri. 11.30am to 2.30pm and Mon. to Sat. 5.30 to 11.30pm. Its uniquely Venetian ambience is probably what makes the Acqua the current "in" place; fine West Coast cuisine with an Italian touch.

★The Harvest, in the Inn on the Park, 1100 Eglinton Avenue; tel. (416) 4442561
Gourmet restaurant with very fine cuisine which can also offer health-conscious diners unusual creations as well.

★Truffles, in the Four Seasons Hotel, 21 Avenue Road; tel. (416) 9287331
Top class restaurant with excellent French and oriental cuisine.

The Lighthouse, revolving restaurant on the 37th floor of the Westin Harbour Castle Hotel, 1 Harbour Square; tel. (416) 8691600
Good, relatively expensive restaurant, with a spectacular all-round view.

Wayne Gretzky's, 99 Blue Jays Way; tel. (416) 979 PUCK
Open daily 11.30am to 11pm. The Canadian ice-hockey star's restaurant is extremely popular but very moderately priced.

Prince Edward Island

★Lord Selkirk (L), in the Prince Edward Hotel, 18 Queen Street (on the waterfront); tel. (902) 5662222
Widely acclaimed for its cuisine, this first class restaurant is the place to meet at lunchtime – especially for the Italian buffet available during the peak summer months – and for brunch on Sundays; be sure to try their home-made cakes and pastries.

Sirenella (M), 83 Water Street; tel. (902) 6282271
Open daily 11.30am to 2pm and 5.30 to 10pm. One of the best Italian places on the island, with a predilection for mussels.

Landmark (B/M), Main Street; tel. (902) 6582286
Open Jun. to Oct. daily 10am to 11pm. Popular place on Blue Heron Drive with excellent salmon dishes and imaginative cheese creations.

Quebec

St-Jovite	La Table Enchantée (M), on Route 117 Lac Duhamel; tel. (819) 4257113 Open Tue. to Sun. 5 to 10pm. A good place to get to know genuine traditional Quebec cuisine, the menu at this "enchanted table" includes veal and pork, poultry and game; with the dessert try the superb maple syrup.

Montreal

★Beaver Club (L), in the Reine Elisabeth Hotel, 900 Boul. René Lévesque Ouest; tel. (514) 8613511
Open daily noon to 3pm and 6 to 11pm. Many visitors praise this as Montreal's top restaurant; it is also a popular meeting place for the city's leading personalities.

★Claude Postel, 443 Rue St-Vincent (near Notre-Dame); tel. (514) 8755067
Open Mon. to Fri. 11.30am to 2.30pm, daily 5.30 to 11pm. The enchanting little restaurant with its excellent cuisine is currently one of the liveliest places in Vieux-Montréal.

Lutétia (M), in Hotel de la Montagne, 1430 Rue de la Montagne; tel. (514) 2885656
Open daily noon to 3pm and 6 to 11pm. Romantic and exuberantly furnished in Empire style, this restaurant's cuisine is French through and through.

★La Marée (L), 404 Place Jacques-Cartier (near Notre-Dame); tel. (514) 8618126
Open Mon. to Fri. noon to 3pm, daily 5.30 to 11.30pm. An atmosphere rather reminiscent of the times of Louis XIV; excellent fish dishes.

Quebec
(city)

L'Ardoise (M), 71 Rue St-Paul; tel. (418) 6940213
Open daily 9am to 11pm. Downtown restaurant, pleasant and absolutely French, which is famous for its very special mussels.

Café du Monde (M), 57 Rue Dalhousie; tel. (418) 6924455
Open daily 11.30am to 11pm. A popular restaurant near the Musée de la Civilisation which produces huge menus, including among their particular delights many kinds of mussels, home-made quiche and sometimes even North African couscous.

★St-Amour (L), 48 Rue Ste-Ursule; tel. (418) 6940667
Open Tue. to Fri. noon to 2.30, daily 6 to 10.30pm. Well-run restaurant with exceptional cuisine worth recommending not only for its French specialities but also for its painstakingly prepared game and unrivalled wine-list.

Serge Bruyère (L), 1200 Rue St-Jean; tel. (418) 6940618
Open Mon. to Fri. noon to 2pm, daily 6 to 10.30pm. Restaurant operating on several levels, ranging from opulent menus to delicious light snacks for tiny appetites.

Saskatchewan

Regina

C.C.Lloyd's, in the Chelton Suites Hotel, 1907 11th Avenue; tel. (306) 5694600
Widely known for its good fish (especially salmon) and its Cajun chicken specialities.

Golf's Steak House, 1945 Victoria Avenue; tel. (306) 5255808
Open Mon. to Fri. 11.30 to 2 and daily 4.30 to 11pm. One of Regina's best
restaurants, diners flock to eat here and relish its salmon and different
varieties of steak.

Cousin Nicos, 1110 Grosvenor Street; tel. (306) 3742020 Saskatoon
Open daily 5 to 11pm. Saskatoon's "Greek" is a great favourite, and
dishes up fine fish as well as Greek salad, tsatsiki, etc.

Traegers, Cumberland Square; tel. (306) 3747881
Open daily 9am to 9pm. Good plain fare and delicious desserts (inc.
Black Forest gâteau and cheesecake).

Yukon Territory

Marina's, 5th Avenue; tel. (867) 9936800 Dawson City
Open daily 11am to 9pm. As ever, this is the top place in town.

Klondike Kate's, 3rd Avenue & King Street; tel. (867) 9936527
Open daily 7am to 11pm. From Klondike Kate you'll get good plain
fare.

The Cellar, in the Edgewater Hotel, 101 Main Street; tel. (867) 6672572 Whitehorse
Open Mon. to Fri. 11.30 to 1 and daily 5 to 10pm. Etiquette still counts
for something in this elegant restaurant, with the best cuisine for miles
around.

Roads

Canada has a very good road system, considering the sheer vastness of
the country. Urban Canada has virtually perfect road cover, with multi-
lane ring-roads encircling the town centres. Generously proportioned
highways connect all the major cities and open up the interior.

All the highways have numbers, and it is these numbers, rather than Road signing
place names, that are the best indication of the route to follow. All are
clearly signposted by the individual provincial highway authority, and
each bears its provincial road number. The TransCanada Highway is also
signposted throughout the ten provinces with the maple-leaf emblem.
Signs to tourist amenities such as picnic sites and camp grounds are
usually white on a brown background (except in Québec where they are
white on blue).

Road classification

Expressways, which are the North American equivalent of Europe's Expressways
urban motorways, are the main roads of metropolitan Canada. They are
the quickest way to cover longer distances in the country's built-up
areas.

Highways are the main trunk roads between the towns and cities. Highways
Although mostly dual carriageway and without junctions, they are the
responsibility of the provincial highway authorities and in more sparsely
populated parts of the country will be graded but also often loose-
surfaced and single carriageway. Secondary Highways are mostly
single carriageway provincial trunk roads, also with a graded road
surface.

TRAFFIC SIGNS

Mandatory Signs

Only those signs which differ considerably
from those customary in Europe are shown

Warning
change of lane

Maximum speed

Warning
Schoolchildren

No right turn at
red traffic light

Cul de sac

No overtaking

No Parking

No stopping

One-way street

No turning in direction indicated

Pedestrian zone

Parking allowed
for 30 minutes

Lane indications

Traffic sign for
drivers turning left

No through road
for dangerous loads

No heavy goods
vehicles

Overtaking lane

Warning Signs

Beware traffic signals

Level-crossing
crossing

Cycle-track
crossing
crossing

Snowmobile
crossing

Maximum speed | Beware of deer, etc. | Bends

Road junction | Cross-roads | Slippery when wet | Maximum height | Steep hill | School-bus turning

Keep in lane | Road narrows | Lane ends | Uneven Carriageway | Maximum speed | DANGER

Drive slowly | Warning roadworks | End of metalled road | Roadworks | Vehicles turning | Diversion

Information

Tourist Information | Boat landing-stage

Hospital | | Provincial Park | Provincial Police | Road number | Signpost

Exit | Signpost

© Baedeker

619

Roads

Distances in kilometres	Calgary	Charlottetown	Edmonton	Fredericton	Halifax	Montréal	Ottawa	Québec	Regina	St. John's	Saskatoon	Thunder Bay	Toronto	Vancouver	Victoria	Whitehorse	Winnipeg	Yellowknife
Calgary		4917	299	4558	5042	3743	3553	4014	764	6183	620	2050	3434	1057	1123	2385	1336	1811
Charlottetown	4917		4949	359	232	1184	1374	945	4163	1294	4421	2878	1724	5985	6051	7034	3592	6460
Edmonton	299	4949		4598	5082	3764	3574	4035	785	6212	528	2071	3455	1244	1310	2086	1357	1511
Fredericton	4558	359	4598		346	834	1024	586	3813	1622	4070	2527	1373	5634	5700	6684	3241	6109
Halifax	5042	232	5082	346		1318	1508	912	4297	1349	4554	3011	1857	6119	6185	7168	3726	6593
Montréal	3743	1184	3764	834	1318		190	270	2979	2448	3236	1693	539	4801	4867	5850	2408	5275
Ottawa	3553	1374	3574	1024	1508	190		460	2789	2638	3046	1503	399	4611	4677	5660	2218	5086
Québec	4014	945	4035	586	912	270	460		3249	2208	3507	1963	810	5071	5137	6120	2678	5546
Regina	764	4163	785	3813	4297	2979	2789	3249		5427	257	1286	2670	1822	1888	2871	571	2297
St. John's	6183	1294	6212	1622	1349	2448	2638	2208	5427		5684	4141	2987	7248	7314	8298	4855	7723
Saskatoon	620	4421	528	4070	4554	3236	3046	3507	257	5684		1543	2927	1677	1743	2614	829	2039
Thunder Bay	2050	2878	2071	2527	3011	1693	1503	1963	1286	4141	1543		1384	3108	3174	4157	715	3582
Toronto	3434	1724	3455	1373	1875	539	399	810	2670	2987	2927	1384		4492	4558	5528	2099	4966
Vancouver	1057	5985	1244	5634	6119	4801	4611	5071	1822	7248	1677	3108	4492		66	2697	2232	2411
Victoria	1123	6051	1310	5700	6185	4867	4677	5137	1888	7314	1743	3174	4558	66		2763	2298	2477
Whitehorse	2385	7034	2086	6684	7168	5850	5660	6120	2871	8298	2614	4157	5528	2697	2763		3524	2704
Winnipeg	1336	3592	1357	3241	3726	2408	2218	2678	571	4855	829	715	2099	2232	2298	3524		2868
Yellowknife	1811	6460	1511	6109	6593	5275	5086	5546	2297	7723	2039	3582	4966	2411	2477	2704	2868	

Tertiary roads are the minor roads linking the different districts, counties, etc., and may often just have metalled surfaces.

These gravel highways are for getting around Canada's remote areas. They are mostly loose-surfaced logging roads, and call for very careful driving. Give way to any enormous juggernauts encountered – a collision could prove fatal.

Road conditions

Canadian road maintenance crews are constantly busy keeping the roads in good repair, and motorists have to comply with their instructions.

There can be some nasty surprises in store for drivers after a prolonged or heavy downpour. This particularly applies to the loose-surfaced roads. Parts of the carriageway can actually be washed away, or turned into treacherous mudslides, depending on the subsoil. The severe Canadian winter and heavy spring rains can mean that even the best of road surfaces will be potholed or hollowed out by the frost.

Besides technical knowledge, several spare tyres, a well-stocked toolkit, sturdy windscreen wipers, broad sticky-tape, a solid towrope and the proper cleaning materials are all very useful. It also pays to have extra protection for headlights and possibly windscreens. Special precautions, such as encasing luggage in plastic bags, should also be taken to prevent dust getting into the vehicle and its contents.
In cold weather motorists should also carry plenty of warm, waterproof clothing and appropriate footwear.

Shopping

Canada's big cities, in particular, offer plenty of opportunity in their wide range of stores for shopping or just looking around.
Ultra-modern shopping malls, such as the Eaton Centre in Toronto or the West Edmonton Shopping Mall, are a maze of boutiques, restaurants, even streams and gardens, housed in arcades and subterranean passages, where it is possible to browse over bargains away from the vagaries of the weather and the extremes of hot or cold.
Anyone who prefers searching for souvenirs in a historic setting can explore the newly converted waterfronts of some Canadian cities, such as Granville Island in Vancouver or Queens Quay in Toronto.
Stores are usually open between 9am and 5.30 or 6pm, and in some of the bigger cities they often stay open until quite late at night, while some neighbourhood stores are also open on Sunday, selling groceries, personal items and newspapers (see also Opening Times).

There are strict limits on the export of objects over 50 years old and of historic, cultural or scientific significance. More precise information can be had from:

The Secretary, Canadian Cultural Property Export Review Board,
Department of Communications,
Ottawa, Ontario, Canada K1A 0C8

Craftwork by Canada's native peoples, the Inuit and the Indians, makes for souvenirs that have a lasting value, such as paintings, carvings and sculpture in the form of masks, soapstone figures and scrimshaw,

with the price depending on the fame and reputation of the particular artist.

It is worth making sure that the work is genuine and Canadian, and not some spurious imitation from the Far East.

Glass and pottery

Well-fashioned glassware and pottery are popular handmade souvenirs of a stay in Canada.

Handmade clothes

Favourite items include knitted or handwoven clothes made by the Canadian Indians such as mittens, heavy-knit Cowichan sweaters and well-lined parkas.

Moccasins

Inuit fur and sealskin boots and Indian moccasins, often trimmed with porcupine quills and glass beads, make memorable and unusual souvenirs.

Traditional clothing

Stetson hats and hand-tooled boots and belts, as well as typically Canadian hunting jackets and lumberjack shirts are also very popular as gifts and mementoes.

Maple syrup

Maple syrup and maple sugar products are very much a speciality of eastern Canada, and calculated to rekindle memories of the country after the holiday.

Alcohol

In Canada alcoholic beverages, including beer, are sold in special government-owned stores (except in Quebec where all grocery stores sell beer and wine). The prices are strictly controlled and the advertising of alcoholic drinks is banned in many places. Drinks manufacturers can only promote themselves as sponsors of cultural and sporting events. See Food and Drink

Sport

Sports

See Canoeing, Cycling, Fishing, Golf, Walking, Winter Sports.

Spectator sports

Canada's favourite spectator sports are ice hockey, baseball and Canadian football, although the original national game, as played by the Indians, is lacrosse.

Ice hockey, or simply hockey, as it's usually called, is to Canadians what football, i.e. soccer, is to Europeans. The top teams, such as the "Calgary Flames", the "Edmonton Oilers", the "Toronto Maple Leafs" and the "Montréal Canadiens" play in the National Hockey League.

Taxes

Provincial sales tax

All provinces except Alberta, the Northwest Territories and the Yukon levy a sales tax, ranging from 6 per cent to 12 per cent, on most items purchased in shops, on food in eating establishments and, in some cases, on hotel and motel rooms. Alberta has a 5 per cent sales tax but it only applies to accommodation. This provincial sales tax is recoverable for visitors, but only in Nova Scotia, Québec and Manitoba.

GST

There is also a general sales tax (GST), which is currently 7 per cent on all goods and services. Visitors may reclaim tax on accommodation and goods purchased and taken out of the country, but GST is not reclaimable on food, drink, tobacco, car hire, transport and motorhomes. To claim rebate complete the reclaim form, attach all receipts, and mail to the address on the form. GST must be claimed before applying for refunds of provincial sales tax.

Taxis

There are plenty of taxicabs in the towns and cities. Fares are usually slightly higher than in Europe.

Telephone

The Canadian telephone network is operated by private companies. International calls can be made directly or you can dial 0 to get the operator.

Public call boxes take coins (min. 25 cents) and/or phone cards.   Public call boxes

Canada's area codes have three numbers. To call a local number dial just the subscriber's number. For long-distance calls dial 1 then the area code and then the subscriber's number.   Dialling codes

The telephone directory for the relevant phone company will have instructions on how to get telephone information.   Information

From private telephones dial 1 then the national code, followed by the area code, and then the subscriber's number. From public telephone boxes dial 0 for the operator who will then give further instructions.   International calls

Australia: 61
Canada/USA: 1
Republic of Ireland: 353
United Kingdom: 44   Dialling codes

A three-minute call to Europe will cost between $1 and $6 depending on the time of day. Cheap rates operate 6pm–8am and at weekends.   Rates

The Canadian telephone companies issue pre-paid telephone cards – which can be used in public call boxes to make long distance calls. They are on sale in all tourist offices. Used in a public call box, they work out much cheaper than making calls directly from your hotel.   Calling cards

Cables can only be sent either direct through the CN (Canadian National) and CP (Canadian Pacific) telegraph offices or they can be given over the telephone.   Telegrams

See entry   Post

Time

Canada is divided into six time zones. These are measured against Greenwich Mean Time.   Time zones

Newfoundland Standard Time	GMT minus 3½ hours
Atlantic Standard Time	GMT minus 4 hours
Eastern Standard Time	GMT minus 5 hours
Central Standard Time	GMT minus 6 hours
Mountain Standard Time	GMT minus 7 hours
Pacific Standard Time	GMT minus 8 hours

The general rule when crossing from one time zone to another travelling across Canada from east to west is to put watches back an hour (half an

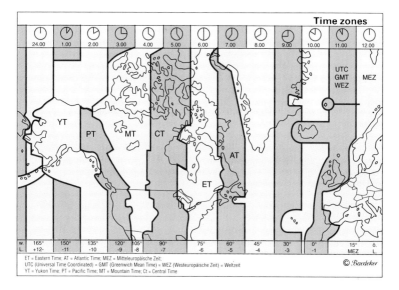

Time zones

ET = Eastern Time; AT = Atlantic Time; MEZ = Mitteleuropäische Zeit;
UTC (Universal Time Coordinated) = GMT (Greenwich Mean Time) = WEZ (Westeuropäische Zeit) = Weltzeit
YT = Yukon Time; PT = Pacific Time; MT = Mountain Time; Ct = Central Time

© Baedeker

hour for Newfoundland), and, clearly, to reverse the process when travelling in the opposite direction.

Daylight Saving Time
Daylight Saving Time (Summer Time) comes into effect in most of Canada on the first Sunday in April each year, when the clocks are advanced by one hour. They then revert to standard time on the last Sunday in October. However, this practice is not observed over most of the province of Saskatchewan, so the transition from Central Daylight Time to Mountain Daylight Time occurs at the Manitoba/Saskatchewan border.

Tipping

Tips or service charges are not usually added to the hotel or restaurant bill in Canada. In restaurants the tip is usually left on the table. As a general rule, a tip of up to 15 per cent of the total amount should be given. This also applies to barbers and hairdressers, taxi drivers, bellhops, doormen, redcaps (porters), etc., at hotels; porters at airports and railway stations generally expect $1 per item of luggage.

Traffic Regulations

Although Canadian traffic rules are basically similar to those found in Europe, they can be different in some respects, and may also vary from province to province. Speed limits tend to be enforced rather more rigorously as well.

Driving licence
A full British driving licence is valid for driving in Canada for up to three months in most provinces. For longer periods, an international driving licence is required as well. An international driving permit is also rec-

1 km = 0,62 mi
1 mi = 1,61 km

© *Baedeker*

ommended for visitors from non-English speaking countries. A US drivers licence is also valid in Canada.

Insurance cover under a vehicle liability insurance policy against liability for bodily injury, death or damage to the property of others is compulsory in all provinces in Canada. The minimum liability insurance requirement is $200,000 except in Québec and the Northwest Territories, where the limit is $50,000.

Third-party insurance

The rule of the road in Canada, as in the United States, is drive on the right. On multi-lane carriageways, outside built-up areas, it is possible to be overtaken on the left or the right, although people tend not to change lanes very often. Any lane-change should be clearly signalled. Overtaking is usually forbidden if there is poor visibility, e.g. on bends, the tops of hills, crossings, etc.

Drive on the right

All speed limits are clearly signposted and are in kilometres per hour. On freeways the limit is 100 k.p.h. (62 m.p.h.), on other routes 90 k.p.h (55 m.p.h.), most rural highways and country roads 80 k.p.h (49 m.p.h.), and in urban/populated areas from 40 to 60 k.p.h. (24 to 37 m.p.h.).

Speed limits

Right turns on a red light are legal, unless otherwise indicated, in all Canadian provinces except Québec. The motorist must come to a full stop at the light but may proceed with caution if the way is clear.

Right turns on red lights

Parking is strictly forbidden on the pavement (sidewalk), in front of fire hydrants, near traffic lights and within 15 m (49 ft) of level crossings.

Parking

School buses are usually painted bright yellow, and it is an offence to overtake them when they are at a standstill with their warning lights flashing. This applies to oncoming traffic as well.

School buses

The use of seat belts by vehicle drivers and all passengers is compulsory throughout Canada. Child restraints are also mandatory in all provinces.

Seat belts

Driving under the influence of alcohol is illegal.

Drink driving

Some Canadian provinces and territories have made it a statutory requirement to drive with vehicle headlights on for extended periods after dawn and before sunset. In the Yukon the law requires drivers to keep their headlights on at all times while driving on the Yukon highways. The use of side (parking) lights alone while driving is contrary to highway statutes.

Headlights

As in Europe, Canada has traffic lights on many crossroads. There are also flashing yellow lights at accident blackspots and on main through roads, and these are a signal to slow down and proceed with care.

Traffic lights

Give way immediately to police cars flashing their lights and sounding their sirens.

Police cars

If followed by a police car with flashing light and siren sounding, pull in immediately, stay in the car and show your driving licence without waiting to be asked. Questioning by the police should be responded to with scrupulous politeness.

Vehicle breakdown

In the event of a breakdown make sure the vehicle is parked where it will not hold up the traffic. Raise the bonnet and fix a white cloth on the driver's side to indicate help is wanted. Emergency telephones are installed on most major trunkroads.

Canadian Automobile Association

The Automobile Association, the Royal Automobile Club, the Royal Scottish Automobile Club, and the Royal Irish Automobile Club are fully affiliated with the Canadian Automobile Association and its member clubs across Canada. Advance information on motoring in Canada can be obtained by members of the AA of Great Britain simply by contacting their head office before departure. In Canada the address is:

Canadian Automobile Association
1145 Hunt Club Road
Ottawa, Ontario, Canada K1V 0Y3

Travel Documents

Entry into Canada

British citizens must have a full valid British passport. A visitor's passport is not accepted. All visitors must also have a return ticket, and sufficient funds to cover their stay. The maximum length of stay is six months, but anyone wanting to stay longer than three months should clear this with the authorities on entry. No vaccinations are currently obligatory.

Visas

British citizens and citizens of the Republic of Ireland do not require a visa to enter Canada, nor is a visa required by citizens of the following countries: Australia, Austria, Belgium, Denmark, Finland, France, Germany, Greece, Iceland, Italy, Japan, Liechtenstein, Luxembourg, Malaysia, Malta, Mexico, Monaco, the Netherlands, New Zealand, Norway, Saudi Arabia, Singapore, Spain, Sweden, Switzerland and the United States. Citizens of many other countries are also exempt from visa requirement, but regulations change frequently. Contact the visa section of the nearest Canadian diplomatic mission for more information.

Canada/US border

No visa is required to cross the Canada/US border provided a full UK passport is held. Visitors will be requested to complete a registration form prior to disembarking by sea or air. If it is a surface crossing, this form will be completed at the border post.

Walking and Trekking

Notwithstanding the fact that Canada is famed in many guises as a walker's paradise, anyone who wants to tackle its vast areas on foot needs to be well equipped and quite experienced.

National and provincial parks are the only areas with well-signed trails where walkers can take relatively danger-free hikes of varying timescales. The park reception centres will usually be able to provide them with all the information they require.

Walking is mostly on trails that are also suitable for children and hence not too strenuous, often in the parks with explanations along the way.

Hiking tends to be for longer day trips, as opposed to leisurely walks or the more strenuous pastimes of trekking and backpacking.

Hitchhiking is not allowed in some parts of Canada, so before doing this it is advisable to check first with the police or the local tourist office.

Hitchhiking

As in Europe, backpacking – taking off on foot into the backwoods just carrying a rucksack – has also become an increasingly popular Canadian pursuit. The necessary maps can be obtained from the Map Office in Ottawa or from one of the licensed shops found in most main towns and cities.

Backpacking

Trekking, taking off for days at a time, can be on horseback, mountain-bike, even with a vehicle, as well as on foot, and often in groups with the help of a local guide. In every case the Canadian wilderness can provide Europeans with challenges of quite a special nature, not least confrontations with dangerous wild animals (see Bears).

Trekking

For safety there are a number of rules which should be observed:
– thoroughly plan trips in advance;
– go for the easier option rather than pressing on to the limits of endurance;
– stick to the established route;
– don't use up all the provisions;
– tell someone where you are going (the park warden, the pilot or a police station, or leave a note on the car windscreen if it is just an impromptu walk), and let them know when you get back;
– watch out for hypothermia;
– take precautions with campfires because of the danger of forest fires;
– take plenty of insect repellent to ward off the black flies and mosquitoes.

Weights and Measures

See Measurements

When to Go

Vast country that it is, Canada experiences widely differing weather as between north and south, not to mention east and west. Hence, in the more southerly parts of the country there are actually four seasons – spring from mid-March to mid to late May, summer from then until the first half of September, followed by fall, to give autumn its transatlantic name, until the onset of winter about mid-November. In the north, particularly Yukon and the Northwest Territories, there are really only two seasons – the cold time of year from October to April, tempered only by the Chinook, or "snow eater", the warm dry southwesterly wind blowing down the eastern slopes of the Rockies, and the warmer weather for the rest of the year. The hottest part of the country is the south-western corner of British Columbia, but it also among the wettest.

Canada's size makes it difficult to give general advice, so it is worth reading the information on particular areas in the section on Climate in the Introduction section. The most pleasant time to visit the far north, other than for specific cold-weather reasons, is from June to August. So far as the rest of Canada is concerned, the best time to travel is between May and October.

May has quite warm days, but is cool at night. Victoria Day weekend, about May 22nd, heralds the start of the travel season. It also signals the

opening of many national and provincial parks, and of tourist information centres throughout the country, as opposed to just those in the main cities. Starting with the west, the milder weather brings on the flowers and trees, and some fog can occur in the Atlantic provinces. June is a good time to travel, while July and August are the hottest months, when most people elect to take to the road. The sun also brings out the mosquitoes, so insect repellent is essential.

September's golden days are still pleasantly warm, but the cool evenings have already set in. The Indian summer at the end of the month and in early October is when the autumn colours are at their best, particularly in the forests of Québec and the Maritimes. By the end of October – earlier in the north – the first of the winter snow and frosts have arrived.

From November to April the bitter cold and heavy winter snowfalls put large parts of Canada out of bounds for most visitors other than winter sports enthusiasts. These will then be in their element in British Columbia and Alberta in the Rockies and in Québec's Laurentian resorts. The snows start to melt in March but skiing can carry on into the milder weather on the higher slopes, with April's warmer weather heralding the summer that is to come.

Winter Sports

Many skiing holiday tour operators recommend Canada as the ideal antidote to the overcrowding of Europe's traditional ski slopes. They are absolutely right. In western Canada, in the Rockies and the mountains along British Columbia's coast, and on the slopes of Ontario and Québec in the east, right through from November to April there is usually plenty of snow, and Europe-style ploughed-up pistes are only found around the big cities such as Québec, Montréal, Calgary and Vancouver. To the novice winter in Canada may simply conjure up images of ice and snow, but for the hardened European skier there is also the lure of the Canadian west, and not just the hectic life of Banff but particularly the remote slopes of the Rockies in Alberta and British Columbia, where heli-skiing is part of the attraction.

Skiing

Canada's ten province's offer skiing, be it downhill or cross-country, to suit just about any visitor, making it a skiers' paradise, ranging from the seemingly endless mountain chains of British Columbia in the west to the superb Laurentian ski-slopes of the east. And the Canadians ensure that there is the après-ski to match!

Many ski-resorts offer good packages, complete with accommodation, food and skipass. Further information on prices, seasons, etc. can be obtained from travel agents.

Ski resorts are not necessarily open seven days a week, so it pays to contact the local tourist office or the actual resort to find out about snow conditions, weather forecasts, opening times, etc.

British Columbia   British Columbia's mountains boast Canada's longest skiing season, from sunny Okanagan to the Rockies and the Alberta border. A few minutes by road from Vancouver is Grouse Mountain, where the fine flood-lit pistes allow night-time skiing. Whistler Village, 125 km (78 mi.) north of Vancouver, has, in Blackcomb mountain, the highest lift-serviced vertical in North America and incredible fall-line runs, while the Okanagan Valley, further east, has four ski resorts with a whole spectrum of pistes. Kootenay in the south has skiing on a variety of slopes without lifts packed to capacity. The scenic splendour of the Rockies also provides

the skier with sun, deep snow and pistes seemingly without end, while for the more ambitious visitor British Columbia offers heli-hiking and snowmobile tours.

Alberta's downhill ski slopes are all in the Jasper and Banff National Parks. Jasper National Park has excellent winter sports facilities and top-class hotels, while located within Banff National Park are three world-class ski resorts offering downhill skiing across the whole range of difficulty, as well as heli-hiking. Besides downhill skiing and all the other Alpine-style activities there are also good cross-country trails in many national and provincial parks, and close to the towns.

Alberta

Both of these northern provinces have landscapes and snow conditions that make them ideal for cross-country skiing. Whitehorse, Yukon, has top cross-country facilities, while there are ski-trails in Yellowknife Park and around Fort Smith, in Northwest Territories. The glaciers in Auyuittuq National Park and on Baffin Island in the north provide winter sport opportunities all year round, although the best conditions are from March onwards, when the days grow longer and powder snow awaits the enthusiast.

Yukon and North-west Territories

Although these two provinces have little downhill skiing there is plenty of cross-country. Most ski resorts are near the towns.

Saskatchewan and Manitoba

Thunder Bay in northern Ontario is a winter sports centre good for both downhill and cross-country skiing, and equally famous for its ski-jumping. Collingwood, north-east of Toronto, has Canada's biggest skilifts. Muskoka, which is north of Toronto, is another ski playground. Cross-country skiing can be enjoyed in and around almost every park and resort area. Details of tours and other outdoor pursuits can be had from Ontario Tourism.

Ontario

Québec Province has everything to gladden the heart of the winter sports fan. It has three major ski regions: the Laurentians, the Eastern Townships (or L'Estrie) and the Greater Québec Area, and over a hundred ski centres, most of them easily accessible from Montréal or Québec City. There are facilities for skiers of all abilities and a stylish variety of après-ski that is very French-Canadian.

Québec

Newfoundland, Nova Scotia, New Brunswick and Prince Edward Island have excellent cross-country skiing, but not much downhill.

Atlantic provinces

Heli-skiing is a sport that is gaining in popularity, particularly with over-seas visitors. An Austrian ski-instructor first chartered a helicopter in the 1960s to take deep snow enthusiasts to the higher regions. Ski-tourists can then master differences in altitude of between 500 and 2500 m (1640 and 8200 ft). This kind of what can hardly be described as environmentally friendly ski-tourism is carried on in several places, including Revelstoke National Park (Peter Schlunegger), Blue River (Mike Wiegele), Golden (Rudi Gertsch) and Panorama (Roger Madson).

Heli-skiing

Anyone wanting to try heli-skiing must be very fit and be experienced when it comes to skiing in deep snow, as well as having the very best equipment and plenty of team spirit.

Youth Hostels

Canada has plenty of low-cost accommodation catering for young people, including youth hostels, YMCAs and YWCAs and college residences (both student and staff).

Canada's 80 youth hostels offer members simple inexpensive accommodation at a cost of between 8 and 20 Can.$ for the night. Hostels are

Youth hostels

Sunshine and Snowfall

Region	Total hours of Sunshine				Annual Snowfall	Snow-cover days
	Juni	Juli	Aug.	Sept.	cm	(days)
British Columbia						
Kamloops	256	316	280	195	67	68
Prince Rupert	151	143	138	117	84	47
Vancouver	238	307	256	183	51	11
Victoria	258	329	274	195	32	3
Alberta						
Banff	204	256	211	163	251	149
Calgary	267	322	282	195	153	116
Edmonton	272	306	277	182	136	133
Lethbridge	284	345	299	214	176	114
Yukon						
Whitehorse	273	250	231	137	100	170
Northwest Territories						
Fort Simpson	281	289	246	134	142	193
Frobisher Bay	175	202	161	82	256	242
Inuvik	375	340	216	109	177	232
Saskatchewan						
Prince Albert	262	296	268	166	122	153
Regina	283	342	295	191	87	134
Saskatoon	294	341	293	191	114	133
Manitoba						
Churchill	234	285	232	111	196	211
Winnipeg	276	316	283	185	126	135
Ontario						
Hamilton	260	288	255	173	109	73
London	244	274	246	173	196	92
Muskoka	263	283	239	169	300	131
Niagara Falls	252	283	253	191	163	39
Ottawa	247	274	243	168	206	121
Sault Ste. Marie	256	288	249	157	305	138
Thunder Bay	262	304	256	168	213	132
Toronto	253	281	252	191	139	73
Québec						
Gaspé / New-Richmond	228	249	225	164	322	165
Montréal	249	275	240	169	243	116
Québec	224	248	219	153	288	146
Ste-Agathe-des-Monts	238	275	237	162	396	154
New Brunswick						
Fredeicton	206	233	221	167	290	119
Moncton	226	243	230	166	301	118
Saint John	203	218	212	166	224	104
Nova Scotia						
Halifax/Dartmouth	221	219	225	180	217	99
Sydney	226	243	226	167	318	101
Yarmouth	211	207	209	176	208	60
Prince Edward Island						
Charlottetown	221	241	218	176	275	122
Newfoundland/Labrador						
Goose Bay	187	200	176	121	445	188
St. John's	187	220	186	147	322	109

found in all larger towns and cities and in some country areas of special tourist interest. Membership, individual or family, is open to everyone; there is no age limit. Intending visitors should take out membership before departure for Canada.

There are YMCA and YWCA hostels in all the bigger cities. Overnight accommodation in a single room costs between 20 and 30 Can.$. In some cases accommodation can be booked in advance prior to leaving for Canada.

YMCA and YWCA hostels

For up-to-date information contact:
Hostelling International Canada, 75 Nicola Street, Ottawa, Ontario K1N 7B9; tel. (613) 2352595, fax (613) 5692131

Information

In the UK:
Youth Hostel Association, 84 Highgate West Hill, London N6 6LU; tel. (0181) 3401831

The Hostelling International handbook is available in bookshops throughout Canada.

International handbook

Young people can find cheap accommodation between May and August in the residences (student and staff) of a great many colleges, where for a small additional charge they can also make use of sports and leisure facilities.

College accommodation

Comprehensive, detailed information can be obtained direct from the college concerned or from the appropriate local or provincial tourist office (see Information).

Index

Abbotsford 98
Acadia 98
Acadian Pioneer Village 387
Adams Lake 264
Agassiz 498
Agawa Canyon 451
Air Travel 564
Aklavik 255
Alaska Highway 100, 557
Alberton 387
Albert Canyon Hot Springs 425
Alberta 102
Alert 199
Alert Bay 507
Alexander Graham Bell National Historic Site 156
Alexander Mackenzie Heritage Trail 163
Algonquin Provincial Park 106
Amherst 478
Anahim Lake 163
Annapolis Royal 107
Annapolis Valley 109
Anse-aux-Sauvages 221
Appalachians 18
Arctic Lowland 22
Armstrong 356
Art History 77
Arthabaska 201
Ashcroft 112
Astontin Lake 197
Athabasca 113
Athabasca Falls 250
Athabasca Glacier 250
Athabasca River 113
Atlantic provinces 90
Arichat 158
Ausuittuq 198
Auyuittuq National Park 116

Baddeck 156
Baffin Island 114
Baie James 117
Bamfield 505
Bancroft 107
Banff 123
Banff National Park 119
Bankhead 126
Banks Island 128
Barkerville 129
Barrhead 286
Bas St-Laurent 130
Bathurst 131
Batoche 132
Batoche National Historic Park 132

Battleford 133
Battleford National Historic Park 133
Battlefords Provincial Park 134
Bears 565
Beaver Creek 102
Bed and Breakfast 568
Belcher Islands 119
Bella Coola 163
Bic 131
Biggson 197
Black Creek Pioneer Village 476
Black Mike's Gold Mine 527
Black's Harbour 217
Blackstone Highlands 187
Blanc-Sablon 171
Blue Heron Drive 388
Blue Mountain 226
Bonaventura 222
Bonavista 134
Bonavista Peninsula 134
Bonne Bay 233
Boucherville 479
Bouctouche 304
Bow Lake 247
Bow Pass 248
Bow Valley 126
Bowron Lake Provincial Park 164
Braeburn Lodge 271
Brandon 136
Brantford 137
Brooks 153
Britannia Beach B.C. Museum of Mining 495
British Columbia 137
Broken Group Islands 510
Buffalo Paddocks 125
Buffalo Pound Provincial Park 393
Burin 142
Burin Peninsula 141
Burlington 241
Burnaby 492
Bus Travel 568
Butchart Gardens 517

Cabano 142
Cabot Trail 158
Cache Creek 112, 161
Calgary 143
Calumet 376
Campbell Highway 153
Campbellton 154
Camping 569

Campobello Island 217
Canada's Wonderland 476
Canadian Shield 16
Canmore 155
Canoeing and Rafting 570
Canora 549
Canyon City 543
Cap Alrith 252
Cap Tourmente 414
Cap-Pelé 304
Cape Bonavista 134
Cape Breton Highlands National Park 159
Cape Breton Island 156
Cape Dorset 115
Cape Merry 169
Cape Scott Provincial Park 508
Cape Smoky 159
Cape Spear National Historic Park 333
Capilano Salmon Hatchery 494
Capilano Suspension Bridge 494
Car Rental 572
Caraquet 159
Carcross 270
Cariboo Highway 160
Carillon 376
Carleton 222
Carmacks 271
Carp Lake Provincial Park 260
Cascade Lookout 244
Castlegar 177
Castle Hill National Historic Park 334
Cathedral Provincial Park 174
Cavendish 388
Cedar Dunes Provincial Park 387
Chaleur Bay Provincial Park 155
Chambly 480
Charlevoix 164
Charlo 155
Charlottetown 165
Château-Richer 413
Chemainus 503
Chéticamp 158
Chetwynd 260
Chicoutimi 428
Chilliwack 167
Chisasibi 118
Christina Lake 176
Churchill 168

Churchill Falls 280
Chûtes Montmorency 412
Chûtes Ste-Anne 414
Clayoquot Sound 506
Clearwater 162, 546
Clearbrook 98
Climate 23
Clinton 161
Coach Tours 95
Cobalt 341
Cochrane 169
Cogagne 304
Columbia Icefield 249
Columbia River 170
Conservation 38
Cordilleras 19
Côte de Beaupré 413
Côte Nord 171
Cottonwood Creek 258
Cow Head 234
Cowichan Lake 503
Craigellachie 264
Cranbrook 179
Creston 178
Crowsnest Highway 172
Crowsnest 181
Cullen Garden 362
Culture 77
Currency 572
Customs Regulations 573
Cut Knife 134
Cut Knife National Historic
   Site 134
Cycling 573
Cypress Hills Provincial
   Park 181
Cypress Provincial Park 494

Dalhousie 155
David Thompson Highway
   248
Dawson City 183
Dawson Creek 100, 260
Deep Cove 495
Deer Island 217
Dempster Highway 187
Desbiens 282
Doukhobor Historic Village
   177
Digby 109
Dinosaur Provincial Park
   153
Diplomatic Representation
   573
Drive through Saint John
   River Valley 434
Drive through the
   Annapolis Valley 109
Drumheller 150
Drummondville 200
Duck Mountain Provincial
   Park 549

Duncan 503

East Arm Fiord 234
Echo Valley Provincial Park
   392
Economy 55
Edam 550
Edelweiss 230
Edmonton 188
Edmundston 434
Education and Science 49
Electricity 573
Elk Falls Provincial Park
   507
Elk Island National Park
   197
Ellesmere Island 198
Ellesmere Island National
   Park Reserve 199
Elmira Provincial Park 269
Emergencies 574
Enchanted Forest 265
Estrie 199
Eureka 199
Events 574

Facts and Figures 10
Famous People 69
Fanshawe Pioneer Village
   289
Faro 154
Fernie 181
Ferries 577
Filling Stations 578
Filming and Photography
   578
Fish Creek 133, 545
Fisheries 292
Fishing 579
Five Finger Rapids 271
Flat Rock 333
Flin Flon 201
Flora and Fauna 32
Florenceville 435
Foam Lake 550
Food and Drink 580
Forest 33
Forest Ecology Trail 451
Forges de St-Maurice 300
Forestry Trunk Road 201
Fort Assiniboine 286
Fort Beauséjour 304
Fort Carlton 202
Fort Chimo 279
Fort Edmonton Park 195
Fort Franklin 231
Fort Gary National Historic
   Park 452
Fort Ingall 142
Fort Langley 203
Fort MacLeod 203
Fort Malden 528

Fort McMurray 205
Fort McPherson 187
Fort Pelly Banks 154
Fort Providence 206
Fort Qu'Appelle 392
Fort Simpson 294
Fort St James 207
Fort St John 208
Fort Steele 208
Fort Walsh National Historic
   Park 182
Fortress Mountain 149
Fraser Canyon 211
Fraser Lake 546
Fraser River Heritage Park
   497
Fraser River Valley 497
Fraser Valley 210
Fredericton 213
French River 456
Fundy Bay 217
Fundy National Park 218

Gabriola 504
Gagetown 216
Garibaldi Provincial Park
   496
Gaspé 221
Gaspésie 220
General 10
Geography 12
Geological formation, Ice
   Age morphology 12
Georgian Bay 223
Getting to Canada 581
Giant's Head 354
Gitanmaks 545
Glace Bay 226
Glacier & Mount Revelstoke
   National Park 227
Glacier National Park 228
Glenburnie 233
Golden 229
Golden Ears Provincial Park
   497
Golden Sands Resort 141
Golf 581
Good Spirit Lake Provincial
   Park 549
Goose Bay 280
Government 51
Granby 200
Grand Bank 142
Grand Falls 435
Grand Forks 176
Grand Manan Island 218
Grand Piles 301
Grand Valley Provincial
   Recreation Park 136
Grand-Mère 300
Grand-Pré 109
Grande-Anse 160

Index

Grande-Vallée 221
Grasslands National Park 230
Granville Ferry 108
Great Bear Lake 231
Great Lakes Forestry Centre 451
Great Slave Lake 231
Green Provincial Park 388
Greenville 543
Greenwood 175
Grenville 376
Gros Morne National Park 232
Grouard 285
Grouse Mountain 494
Gwillim Lake 260

Habitation Port-Royal 109
Hagwilget 276
Haida 416
Haines Junction 102
Halcyon 425
Halifax 234
Hamilton 240
Hanna 152
Harbour Grace 333
Harper Mountain 263
Harrison Hot Springs 498
Harrison Mills 497
Hartland 435
Hay River 242
Hazeltons 275
Head-Smashed-In Buffalo Jump 204
Heart's Content 333
Hebron 281
Helmcken Falls 547
Hill National Historic Park 517
Hillard's Bay Provincial Park 285
Hillsborough 303
History 63
Holman 518
Hoodoos 152
Hope 242
Hope Slide 243
Hopedale 281
Hopewell Cape 303
Horseshoe Bay 494
Hotels and Motels 583
Howe Sound 495
Hudson Bay 244
Hudson's Hope 261
Hull 245
Hunlen Falls 163
Hunting 599
Huntsville 323
Hyder 544

Icefields Parkway 247

Île Bonaventure 222
Île d'Anticosti 172
Île d'Orléans 411
Île du Cap aux 252
Île du Havre aux 252
Île du Havre-Albert 252
Île Madame 158
Îles de la Madeleine 251
Indians and Inuit 600
Information 600
Ingonish 159
Inside Passage 252
Insurance 602
Inuvik 253
Invermere 180
Iqaluit 116
Iqaluktuutiak 517

Jack Minor Sanctuary 528
Jasper 257
Jasper National Park 255
Jasper Park Lodge 258
John Hart–Peace River Highway 259
Johnston Canyon 126
Joliette 262
Jonquière 429

Kakabeka Falls 460
Kamloops 262
Kamloops Waterslide & Vacation Land 263
Kamouraska 131
Kananaskis Valley 149
Katepwa Provincial Park 392
Kawartha Lakes 361
Kelowna 354
Kenora 283
Keremeos 174
Kilby Provincial Historic Park 497
Killarney Provincial Park 456
Kimberley 180
King's Landing 435
Kings Byway Drive 389
Kingston 265
Kiosk 107
Kirkland Lake 341
Kispiox Village 546
Kitchener-Waterloo 267
Kitimat 541
Kitselas Canyon 543
Kitwancool 544
Kitwanga 543
Kleinburg 476
Klondike 269
Klondike Highway 186, 557
Kluane National Park 271
Kokanee Creek Provincial Park 178

Kokanee Glacier Provincial Park 178
Kootenay Crossing 275
Kootenay National Park 272
Kouchibouguac National Park 304
'Ksan 275
'Ksan Indian Village 276

L'Anse Amour 279
L'Anse aux Meadows National Historic Park 111
L'Outaouais 374
La Baie 428
La Malbaie 165
La Mauricie 300
La Pocatière 130
La Tuque 301
Labrador City 280
Labrador current 279
Labrador 277
Labrador Straits 279
Lac Bras d'Or 156
Lac La Biche 281
Lac La Hache 162
Lac Le Jeune Resort 263
Lac Megantic 281
Lac St-Jean 282
Lachine 320
Lady Slipper Drive 387
Ladysmith 503
Lake Agnes 128
Lake Louise 127
Lake Minnewanka 126
Lake Newell 153
Lake of the Woods 282
Lakelse Lake Provencial Park 540
Lang Century Village Museum 378
Language 602
Laurentians 283
Laurentides 284
Lauzon 415
Lavallée Lake 381
Lava Lake 541
Le Désert 456
Lebret 392
Lennox Island 387
Lenoir Museum 158
Les Escoumines 457
Lesser Slave Lake 285
Lesser Slave Lake Provincial Park 285
Lethbridge 287
Lévis 130, 415
Lillooet 496
Lindsay 361
Lions Gate Bridge 494
Little Manitou Lake 550

Little Qualicum Falls Provincial Park 505
Lloydminster 288
Lobster Cove Head 234
Lodges 602
Logy Bay 332
London 288
Long Beach 506
Lonsdale Quay 494
Loon Lake 551
Louisbourg 290
Lundbreck Falls 181
Lunenburg 291
Lynn Canyon Park 495
Lytton 213, 497

Mackenzie 260
Mackenzie Delta 293
Mackenzie District 292
"Mackenzie Garden" 294
Mackenzie Highway 293
Mackenzie Mountains 293
Mackenzie River 293
MacMillan Provincial Park 505
Mactaquac Provincial Park 436
Magog 200
Maligne Canyon 258
Maligne Lake 259
Mallorytown Landing National Park 267
Malpeque 388
Malpeque Bay 388
Manitoba 91, 295
Manning Park Resort 243
Manning Provincial Park 243
Maple Ridge 497
Mara Reserve 361
Marble Canyon 275
Margaree Harbour 158
Marine Drive 332
Marmot Basin 259
Marsh Loop 125
Marten Mountain 285
Marten River 340
Marystown 141
Masset 416
Masson 376
Matane River 220
Matapédia 223
Mauricie National Park 300
Measurements 602
Medical Services 603
Medicine Hat 301
Medicine Lake 259
Meziadin Lake 544
Miette Hot Springs 259
Midland 223
Minas Basin 478

Miner's Junction 154
Mingan National Park 172
Miguasha Peninsula 223
Mimac Indian Village 389
Minto 271
Mission 302
Mississauga 476
Mistaya Canyon 248
Moisie 279
Moncton 302
Mont Gabriel 284
Mont Tremblant 284
Mont-St-Hilaire 480
Mont-St-Pierre 221
Montebello 376
Montréal 305
Montréal Laurentians 283
Moose Jaw 321
Moosonee 322
Moraine Lake 128
Moresby Island 417
Moricetown Canyon 546
Mortier Bay 141
Mount Cavell 259
Mount Hays 391
Mount Logan 272
Mount Mackenzie 425
Mount Norquay 125
Mount Revelstoke National Park 229
Mount Robson Provincial Park 547
Mount Seymour Provincial Park 495
Mount Whymper 275
Mount Whitehorn 128
Mt Allen 149
Muskoka 323

Nahanni National Park 323
Nain 281
Nakiska 149
Nakusp 425
Naikoon Provincial Park 416
Nanaimo 503
Nanisivik 116
Nanoose Bay 504
National Parks 601
Nelson 177
Netley Marsh 453
New Aiyansh 543
New Brunswick 325
New Westminster 492
Newfoundland 327
Niagara 334
Niagara Falls 334
Niagara-on-the-Lake 337
Norris Point 233
North Avalon 332
North Bay 340
North Labrador 280
North Star Mountain 180

North Sydney 157
North Vancouver 494
Northern Vancouver Island 507
Northern Woods and Water Route 343
Northwest Passage 341
Northwest Territories 343
Note 98
Nouveau Québec 118
Nova Scotia 347
Nugget Route 495
Nunavut 350

Ogilvie Mountains 187
100 Mile House 162
Oka 376
Okanagan 352
Oliver 353
Ontario 90, 357
Ontario Agricultural Museum 476
Opening Hours 603
Orillia 361
Oshawa 362
Osoyoos 174
Othello-Quintette Tunnels Historic Park 362
Ottawa 363
Ouimet River 460
Outfitters 603
Outskirts 241
Owen Sound 225

Pacific Rim National Park 509
Paint Pots 275
Pangnirtung 116
Panther Falls 248
Papineau–Labelle Reserve 375
Parc de la Gaspésie 220
Parc de Métis 220
Parc du Mont Ste-Anne 284
Parc du Mont-Orford 200
Parc du Mont-Ste-Anne 415
Parc National de Forillon 221
Park Paul-Sauvé 375
Parker Ridge 248
Parks, National and Provincial 603
Parksville 504
Parlee Beach Provincial Park 304
Parrsboro 478
Peace Canyon Dam 261
Peace River 376, 377
Peachland 354
Peel River 187
Peggy's Cove 240
Pemberton 496

Penetanguishene 225
Penticton 353
Percé 221
Péribonca 282
Peter Lougheed Provincial
  Park 149
Peterborough 377
Petroglyph Park 504
Peyto Lake 248
Pike Lake Provincial Park
  550
Pincher Creek 181
Pine Pass 260
Pitt River 497
Plain of Six Glaciers 128
Plaisance 376
Pocahontas 259
Point Pelee National Park
  378
Population 41
Port Alberni 505
Port Carling 323
Port de la Joie 389
Port Edward 539
Port Essington 540
Port Hardy 508
Port Hawkesbury 156
Port Moody 492
Port Simpson 391
Port Union 135
Port-au-Persil 165
Port-Cartier 171
Portage la Prairie 379
Portugal Cove 333
Post 604
Poste de la Baleine 118
Pouch Cove 333
Povungnituk 119
Prescott 380
Prescott House Greenwich
  109
Prince Albert 380
Prince Albert National Park
  381
Prince Edward Island 382
Prince Edward Island
  National Park 388
Prince George 389
Prince Rupert 390
Principal Sights of Tourist
  Interest 637
Provincial Forest 341
Public Holidays 605
Public Transport 606
Pukaskwa National Park 391
Punchbowl Falls 259

Qu'Appelle Valley 392
Québec (City) 397
Québec (Province) 90, 393
Queen Charlotte Islands
  415

Quesnel 163
Quetico Provincial Park 460
Quill Lakes 550

Radio and Television 606
Radium Hot Springs 275
Rail Journeys 92
Rail Travel 606
Rainbow National
  Conservation Area 163
Ranch and Farm Holidays
  607
Rathtrevor Beach Provincial
  Park 505
Rearguard Falls 547
Red Bay 280
Redwall Fault 275
Regina 418
Religion 46
Repulse Bay 422
Réservoir Manicouagan
  423
Restaurants 610
Revelstoke Canyon Dam
  425
Revelstoke 424
Richmond 492
Rideau Canal 425
Riding Mountain National
  Park 426
Rimouski 131
Rivière-au-Renard 221
Rivière-du-Loup 131
Rivière-Eternité 428
Roads 617
Rockton 241
Rogers Pass 425
Ross River 154
Round Tours by Car 90
Route 102 216
Royal Hudson Steam Train
  494
Rubble Creek 496
Rushing River Provincial
  Park 283

Saguenay 427
Saint John 429
Saint John River Valley 434
Saint John's 436
Saint-Tite 301
Sainte-Anne-de- Bellevue
  321
Sainte-Placide 376
Sally's Cove 234
Salmo 178
Salmon Arm 264
Saskatchewan 91, 442
Saskatoon 447
Sault Ste Marie 449
Sault-au-Récollet 321
Schefferville 278

Searchmont 451
Selkirk 452
Sept-Chûtes 415
Sept-Îles 171, 278
Séraphin 284
Shannon Falls 496
Shaw's Point 286
Shawinigan 300
Shediac 304
Sherbrooke 200
Shopping 621
Shuswap Lakes 264
Sibley Provincial Park 459
Sicamous 264
Silver City 127
Simpson Lake 154
Sinclair Canyon 275
Sioux Narrows 283
Ska Nah Doht Indian Village
  289
Skagit Valley 243
Skagway 270
Slave Lake 286
Sleeping Giant 460
Smithers 546
Sorel 479
Sorrento 264
South Avalon 333
South Nahanni River 324
Spences Bridge 112
Sport 622
Springhill 478
Squamish 495
St Albert 197
St Andrews 217
St Elias Mountains 272
St Joseph Island 451
St Lawrence 142
St Lawrence Lowland 18
St Lawrence Waterway 439
St Mary's River 441
St Paul's 234
St Peters 158
St Stephen 217
St Thomas 289
St Walburg 550
St-Benoît- du-Lac 200
St-Eustache 375
St-Félicien 282
St-François 412
St-Jean 412
St-Jean-Port-Joli 130
St-Jérome 284
St-Jovite 284
St-Laurent 411
St-Ours 480
St-Pierre 412
St-Roch-des-Aulnaies 130
St-Sauveur-des-Monts 284
Stagleap Provincial Park
  178
Stanley Glacier 273

Stawanus Chief 496
Ste-Adèle 284
Ste-Agathe-des-Monts 284
Ste-Anne de Beaupré 413
Ste-Anne-des-Monts 220
Ste-Famille 412
Ste-Flavie 131
Ste-Pétronille 411
Ste-Rose-du-Nord 429
Stewart 544
Stewart Cassiar Highway 543
Stewart Crossing 271
Stratford 289
Strathcona Provincial Park 507
Suggested routes 85, 100, 109, 154, 187, 299, 300, 332, 387, 434, 446, 478
Sudbury 453
Sulluk 119
Sulphur Mountain 125
Summerland 354
Sunbury-Oromocto Provincial Park 216
Sunshine Region 126
Sunwapta Falls 250
Sunwapta Pass 249
Swan Hills 286
Sydney 157

Tadoussac 456
Takhini Hot Springs 271
Tatla Lake 162
Taxes 622
Taxis 623
Telephone 623
Terra Nova National Park 457
Terrace 540
Teslin Lake 100
Thessalon 451
Thetis Island 503
Thompson River 213
Thousand Islands National Park 266
Three Valley Gap 265
Thunder Bay 457
Thurso 376
Timagami Lake 340
Time 623
Timmins 460
Tipping 624

Tobermory 226
Tod Mountain 263
Tofino 506
Top of the World Highway 186, 557
Toronto 461
Traffic Regulations 624
TransCanada Highway 85, 446
Transport and Telecomunications 61
Travel Documents 626
Trent & Severn Canal 362
Trinity 135
Trois-Rivières 477
Trou de la Fée 282
Trout River 233
Truro 477
Tuktut Nogait National Park 255
Tunnel Mountain 126
Tweedsmuir Provincial Park 163, 546

Ucluelet 506
Ukrainian Cultural Heritage Village 198
Ungava Bay 279
Uniacke House 239
Union Station 463
University of Alberta 195
Upper Canada Village 478

Val-Jalbert 282
Vallée Richelieu 479
Vancouver 480
Vancouver Game Farm 498
Vancouver Island 498
Vaseux Lake Provincial Park 353
Veregin 549
Vermilion Lakes 125
Vermilion Pass 273
Vernon 356
Victoria 510
Victoria Island 517
Village Historique Acadien 159
Village Huron 411
Virginia Falls 325

W.A.C. Bennett Dam 261
Wabush 280

Walking and Trekking 626
Walter Wright Pioneer Village 261
Wanuskewin Heritage Park 449
Wasaga Beach 225
Waskaganish 118
Waskesiu Lake 382
Waterton–Glacier International Peace Park 518
Watson Lake 100, 154
Welland Canal 441, 522
West Canada 91
West Coast Trail 510
Western Brook 234
Wetaskiwin 198
When to Go 627
Whistler 496, 524
Whistlers Mountain 258
Whitehorse 524
Whycocomagh 156
Whycocomagh Provincial Park 156
Williams Lake 162
Windsor 110, 527
Winnipeg 528
Winter Sports 628
Writing-on-Stone Provincial Park 287
Wood Buffalo National Park 537
Woodstock 435
Woody Point 233
Wynyard 550

Yale 211
Yellowhead Highway 539
Yellowhead Highway in Saskatchewan 549
Yellowhead Pass 548
Yellowknife 551
Yoho National Park 553
York 388
York Redoubt 239
Yorkton 549
Youth Hostels 629
Yukon Circle Route 557
Yukon River 558
Yukon Territory 557

Zuckerberg Island Heritage Park 177

Principal Sights of Tourist Interest

★★

Alaska Highway	100
Annapolis Royal	107
Annapolis Valley	109
L'Anse aux Meadows National Park	111
Banff National Park	119
Barkerville	129
Batoche National Historic Park	132
Bonavista Peninsula	134
Calgary	143
Cape Breton Island	156
Caraquet	159
Crowsnest Highway	172
Cypress Hills Provincial Park	181
Edmonton	188
Fort MacLeod	203
Fort McMurray	205
Fort St James	207
Fraser Valley	210
Fundy Bay	217
Gaspésie	220
Georgian Bay	223
Gros Morne National Park	232
Halifax	234
Hull	245
Icefields Parkway	247
Jasper National Park	255
Kingston	265
Kluane National Park	271
Kootenay National Park	272
'Ksan	275

★★

Laurentides	284
Louisbourg	290
Lunenburg	291
La Mauricie	300
Moncton	302
Montréal	305
Muskoka	323
Nahanni National Park	323
Niagara	334
Okanagan	352
Ottawa	363
Point Pelee National Park	378
Prince Albert National Park	381
Prince Edward Island	382
Québec (City)	397
Regina	418
Réservoir Manicouagan	423
Riding Mountain National Park	426
Saint John's	436
Toronto	461
Upper Canada Villa	478
Vancouver	480
Vancouver Island	498
Victoria	510
Waterton–Glacier International Peace Park	518
Winnipeg	528
Yellowknife	551
Yoho National Park	553

★

Algonquin Provincial Park	106
Bas St-Laurent	130
Battleford	133
Brandon	136
Brantford	137
Cabano	142
Campbellton	154
Cariboo Highway	160
Charlottetown	165
Churchill	168
Cochrane	169
Côte Nord	171
Dawson City	183
Estrie	199
Fort Langley	203
Fort Providence	206
Fredericton	213
Glacier & Mount Revelstoke National Park	227
Grasslands National Park	230
Great Slave Lake	231
Hamilton	240
Hay River	242
Hope	242
Îles de la Madeleine	251

★

Inside Passage	252
Inuvik	253
John Hart–Peace River Highway	259
Kamloops	262
Klondike	269
Labrador	277
Lac St-Jean	282
Lethbridge	287
Lloydminster	288
London	288
Manitoba	295
Medicine Hat	301
Moosonee	322
Newfoundland	327
North Bay	340
Orillia	361
Oshawa	362
L'Outaouais	374
Peterborough	377
Portage la Prairie	379
Prince Rupert	390
Queen Charlotte Islands	415
Revelstoke	424
Saint John	426

(Continued on p. 639)

Principal Sights of Tourist Interest

(*Continued from page 638*)

(*Continued from page 638*)

★

Saint John River Valley	434
Saskatchewan	442
Saskatoon	447
Sault Ste Marie	449
Selkirk	452
Sudbury	453
Tadoussac	456

★

Terra Nova National Park	457
Thunder Bay	457
Welland Canal	522
Whitehorse	524
Wood Buffalo National Park	537
Yellowhead Highway	539

For reasons of space only the most important locations in Canada that are worth visiting, either for themselves or for interesting places in the vicinity, can be included in the above list. In the A to Z section will be found many other sights distinguished by one or two stars that are worthy of a visit.

Imprint
166 colour photographs, 74 maps, plans and drawings, 1 general map, 1 large map at end of book

Original German text: Dr Bernard Abend, Monika I. Baumgarten, Annette Bickel, Gisela Bockcamp, Birgit Borowski, Heinz Burger, Dr Helmut Eck, Rainer Eisenschmid, Brigitte and Elmar Engel, Carmen Galenschovski, Mattias Gaul, Görres Grenzdörffer, Prof. Dr Hassenpflug, Dr Cornelia Hermanns, Prof. Dr Alfred Herold, Germering Klein, Barbara Kreissel, Markus Kunz, Helmut Linde, Martina Melk, Dr Christina Melk-Haen, Dr Roland Metz, Dr Madeleine Reineke, Dr Georg Scherm, Inge Scherm, Anja Schliebitz, Rotraut Schönleber, Jutta Seeberger, Claudia Smettan, Lydia Störmer, Reinhard Strüber, Beate Szerelmy, Andrea Wurth, Reinhard Zakrzewski, Dagmar Zimmermann

Editorial work: Baedeker-Redaktion (Helmut Linde)
General direction: Rainer Eisenschmid, Baedeker Stuttgart

Cartography: Christoph Gallus, Hohberg-Niederschopfheim; Franz Kaiser, Sindelfingen; Gert Oberländer, Munich, Travel Alberta, Edmonton; MapArt, Brampton; Mairs Geographischer Verlag, Ostfildern-Kemnat (large map)

English translation: Wendy Bell, David Cocking, Brenda Ferris (Babel Translations), Julie Waller

Source of Illustrations: Anderson (1); Archiv (5); Baumgarten (1); Beaulieu (1); Beedell (2); Bickell (1); Burger (6); Cochrane (1); Engel (30); Herold (10); Historia (1); Hydro-Québec (1); Jaraush (4); Klein (1); Law (3); Linde (26); McClosky (1); Parks Canada (2); Saint Jacques (1); Schäfer (3); Schäffer (1); Scherm (28); Stehle (1); Tourism Canada (13); Tourism Nova Scotia (3); Tourism Ottawa (1); Tourisme Québec (8); Tourism Saskatchewan (2); Ullstein (1); Walker (3); Zeruk (2)

Front cover: Images Colour Library. Back cover: AA Photo Library (J. Davidson)

3rd English edition 1999

© Baedeker Stuttgart
Original German edition 1999

© 1999 The Automobile Association
English language edition worldwide

Published by AA Publishing (a trading name of Automobile Association Developments Limited, whose registered office is Norfolk House, Priestley Road, Basingstoke, Hampshire RG24 9NY. Registered number 1878835).

Distributed in the United States and Canada by:
Fodor's Travel Publications, Inc.
201 East 50th Street
New York, NY 10022

A CIP catalogue record of this book is available from the British Library.

Licensed user:
Mairs Geographischer Verlag GmbH & Co.
Ostfildern-Kemnat bei Stuttgart

Printed in Italy by G. Canale & C. S.p.A., Turin

ISBN 0 7495 2084 1